DON'T BE AFRAID . . . .

Variety is the spice of life, and there is no end to it in this titillating and imaginative book. Discovering the answers to questions such as these will be almost as much fun as performing them:

• What is the Chinese Basket Trick?
• What sex expert recommends ice cream for an unforgettable sexual experience?
• How many different types of the world-renowned Venus Butterfly are there?
• What astonishing idea for hotel room improvisation did *Playboy* refuse to publish in the Advisor?
• How can a packet of Alka-Seltzer be put to effective sexual use?
• How can two sticks of butter and a room service cart provide a very erotic evening?
• What are the props necessary for the Flying Philadelphian?

365
WAYS TO IMPROVE
YOUR SEX LIFE

JAMES R. PETERSEN has written and edited the Playboy Advisor column for the past 22 years. As *Playboy*'s resident expert on sex, he has appeared regularly on talk shows and lectured at hundreds of colleges, doing what he terms "stand-up sex therapy."

365
WAYS TO IMPROVE YOUR SEX LIFE

From the Files of the PLAYBOY ADVISOR

James R. Petersen

A PLUME BOOK

PLUME
Published by the Penguin Group
Penguin Books USA Inc., 375 Hudson Street,
New York, New York 10014, U.S.A.
Penguin Books Ltd, 27 Wrights Lane,
London W8 5TZ, England
Penguin Books Australia Ltd, Ringwood,
Victoria, Australia
Penguin Books Canada Ltd, 10 Alcorn Avenue,
Toronto, Ontario, Canada M4V 3B2
Penguin Books (N.Z.) Ltd, 182–190 Wairau Road,
Auckland 10, New Zealand

Penguin Books Ltd, Registered Offices:
Harmondsworth, Middlesex, England

First published by Plume, an imprint of Dutton Signet,
a division of Penguin Books USA Inc.

First Printing, April, 1996
10 9 8 7 6 5 4

 REGISTERED TRADEMARK—MARCA REGISTRADA

LIBRARY OF CONGRESS CATALOGING-IN-PUBLICATION DATA

365 ways to improve your sex life : from the files of the Playboy
    advisor / [edited by] James R. Petersen
        p. cm.
    ISBN 0-452-27576-8
    1. Sexual excitement. 2. Sex. 3. Sex instruction. I. Petersen.
    James R. II. Playboy.
HQ31.A17 1996
613.9'6—dc20   95-20524
                                                        CIP

Printed in the United States of America
Set in Cheltenham Book
Designed by Leonard Telesca

This book is dedicated to
Susan,
who needs no advice.

Contents

Introduction

I have written and edited the Playboy Advisor column for over twenty years. The magazine's staff of experts tries to answer anyone who has a reasonable question—from fashion, food and drink, stereos, and sports cars to dating dilemmas, taste, and etiquette. But most of the time the column deals with sexual problems—premature ejaculation, penises that bend to the right, penises that are too short or too long, women who don't reach orgasm from intercourse, partners who have different levels of desire, the usual. But the column also regularly provides moments of pure pleasure.

A few years ago the scriptwriters for the TV show *L.A. Law* introduced a running gag into the show: The character Stuart Markowitz (played by Michael Tucker) talked about a sexual technique he had learned from a client that was called the "Venus Butterfly." The technique, which was never described on the show, supposedly brought women to peaks of pleasure never before experienced.

Hundreds of viewers called the Playboy Advisor to find out if there was a real Venus Butterfly. Since the scriptwriters had made up the name, and nothing more, we decided to host a contest. We asked our readers to write in their favorite sex techniques—to describe a moment that deserved to be known as the Venus Butterfly—and we printed them.

Long before there was an Internet, the Playboy Advisor was an interactive forum devoted to sex. We learned from our readers, our readers learned from our readers, and now you will, too. Every month we tried to include a letter from someone that described a peak sexual experience, an inspired bit of sexual experimentation. Readers wrote in with oral sex tips, room service sex tricks, and erotic tool kit inventories. If they encountered a sexual reference in a literary work that they particularly liked, they tore the page out and sent it to the Advisor.

Clearly America has an appetite for sex tricks. Scott Turow made an offhand reference to a sex trick called the Marble Peach, and curious readers wrote the Playboy Advisor. The author of a new biography of the Duchess of Windsor claimed that she was expert at a pleasure technique known as Fang Chung, and readers asked for details. (You'll find the answers here.)

The notion that every time we open our mail we might discover something we can use in our private life is one of the prime pleasures of working on the column. When we collected ten years of advice in a book called *The Playboy Advisor on Love and Sex*, our favorite chapter was the one devoted to "Secret Oriental Sex Techniques We Learned from Our Toyota Mechanic." (Some of those are reprinted here.)

But it wasn't until recently that we realized our once-a-month offering wasn't enough to meet the appetite for sex tricks. When the column described the Crème de Menthe Blow Job, a technique we found in *Tricks: More Than 125 Ways to Make Good Sex Better* by Jay Wiseman, hundreds of readers wrote asking how they might obtain the book. The problem: The guide was a self-published manuscript sold in erotic boutiques, information as sex toy. And when our circulation department offered a brochure called "*Playboy*'s Secrets of Super Sex," thousands of people wrote in for it. Clearly there is a craving for sexual information that goes beyond the basics.

One of the catalysts for this book was the much-heralded University of Chicago survey of sex in America.

The survey made news despite—or perhaps because—it made sex seem so bland. With questions such as "Do you find vaginal intercourse appealing?" what did you expect?

"Yes, I find vaginal intercourse appealing, especially when my partner is on top wearing a leather mask she borrowed from Madonna, we're in a hotel room, and room service has just delivered the secret ingredient to the Venus Butterfly."

One of the most startling findings of the survey was that the people answering made love only once a week. Enough? Depends on what they did that one time. Was it making love in a tree house? Finding a novel use for a rawhide bootlace?

Statistics, we have learned, hide the astonishing, the unique, the memorable aspects of sex. Surely there's more to sex than numbers.

There is a major difference between sex books that help cure problems and sex books that add fuel to the fire. Masters and Johnson's research was excellent, but it was *The Joy of Sex* that everyone kept by their bed. (*The Joy of Sex* was recently reissued—new drawings, same tricks. But also, an even older book of sex tricks, the *Kama Sutra*, has been reincarnated.)

For the past twenty years, every sex book published in America has crossed my desk. My bookshelf is about to collapse with the collected wisdom of M.D.s, Ph.D.s, R.N.s, therapists, feminists, fantasists, and sexual explorers. Part of this book is a tribute to my sources. I have discovered that even the most serious authors can't resist sharing a sex trick or two, and they've changed over the years—like maps of Europe. We Americans are tinkerers. Like the character played by Tim Allen in *Home Improvement*, we want more power. (Not all sex tricks are successful: I've included one or two sexual pratfalls, with warnings.)

We have many sources of sexual expertise: This book borrows from porn films and women's erotica collections. Artists seek novel acts and novel settings—and remarkable things can happen in the safe atmosphere of a studio or work of fiction.

And I turned to the Internet for ideas. *Playboy* has a web site on which I placed a description of this project. I asked for peak experiences and secret turn-ons. Did place matter? Taking the sexual revolution out of the bedroom and into elevators, choir lofts, tree houses, balconies, and pickup trucks seems to have provided some incredible memories.

After collecting all these vignettes, I realized that there were common themes. Many of the tricks are simply means of focusing erotic awareness. At one extreme you have a hand grazing across the downy hairs along the spine; at the other you have sexual utensils that border on S&M. Anything that produces adrenaline—the threat of discovery or the challenge of doing something you've never done before—can produce memorable sex. When I read some of these letters and postings I can almost see the slide drop into the memory projector. This image will last forever.

What we have here are sexually adventurous people sharing secrets. They may work for you; they may not. In any event, they are simply fun. I could have organized them by topic, but that's not how most of us experience sex. So I simply numbered them, in no particular order, *365 Ways to Improve Your Sex Life*, one for every day of the year (I thought of calling this *The Year of Living Sexually*). If you like, you can try doing them all in one intense weekend. Or you can prolong the pleasure over two or more years. Ramble through, enjoy.

Acknowledgments

The Advisor column has always been a collaborative effort. I would like to thank Arthur Kretchmer, Barbara Nellis, Jonathon Black, Asa Baber, John Rezek—all *Playboy* staffers—and Michael Castleman and Marty Klein (the Advisor's advisors) for years of creative input. The Advisor would not exist without the frontline efforts of Lynn Strom and Mike Ostrowski, the correspondents in Reader Service who deal with the public directly. Gloria Napier, Kim Erwin, Patricia Lewis, and Terry Glover have helped get copy to the computer. Thanks to Eileen Kent for the Web Page, Sarah Lazin for finding a home for this book, and Arnold Dolin for sharing in the enthusiasm.

1. Sex Is . . .

This is a test. I found it in *Allies in Healing* by Laura Davis.

> Sit down with a piece of paper and write down what sex is for you. Include everything. Write for ten minutes and don't censor yourself. Just keep writing the sentence "Sex is . . ." and complete each one.

Davis asks partners to complete the exercise, then compare notes. Her goal: to show that sex has different meanings for different people.

Here's my list:

Sex is adventure.
Sex is a form of enthusiasm.
Sex is sweat equity in a relationship.
Sex is recognition.
Sex is the creation of memory.
Sex is being inside out there.
Sex is the comparing of notes.
Sex is the great equalizer, the opposite of power.
Sex is power made playful. Sex is where I lose myself. Sex is where I find myself.
Sex is fantasy made fact.
Sex is adult. If it weren't for sex, we would never leave home.
Sex is the free exchange of energy.
Sex is detail.
Sex is creative.
Sex is a liquid.

Sex is a gas.

Sex is the most fun you can have in your office with the door open.

Sex is love. Sex is something else.

Sex is a chuckle.

Sex is not without consequence. If it were, what man or woman would bother?

2. Say Good-bye to the Same Old Same Old

If you read sex manuals, you get the impression that everybody is doing everything and enjoying it all. Yet I've found that inevitably my partner likes some things better than others. Are there any general guidelines for sexual preferences?

—H.G., Los Angeles, California

We tend to avoid generalities, but we came across an interesting claim in The Book of Sex Lists *by Albert B. Gerber. According to the Association for Research, Inc., the ten sexual activities preferred by heterosexual women (in order of preference) are: "(1) Gentle cunnilingus (on the clitoris) by a man (much emphasis on the gentle); (2) gentle finger stimulation of the clitoris by a man; (3) sexual intercourse on top of a man; (4) sexual intercourse in a variety of changing positions; (5) receiving cunnilingus (gentle, of course) while performing fellatio (sixty-nine); (6) massaging a man all over; (7) masturbating a man; (8) being petted, kissed, and stimulated manually and orally by two men, culminating in intercourse with one man while the other*

alternates between gently stroking the clitoris and the nipples; (9) masturbation; (10) performing simple fellatio."
The key word, in case you missed it, is "gentle." We can
see Billboard *publishing a weekly chart: "And number 5*
with a bullet . . ." For comparison, the top ten sexual activities listed for heterosexual men (in order of preference)
are: "(1) Fellatio by a woman to orgasm; (2) intercourse
with a woman in a variety of positions, changing from time
to time; (3) nude encounters with two women in a variety
of activities changing from time to time; (4) petting the
breasts of a woman; (5) anal intercourse with a woman;
(6) performing cunnilingus while the woman is performing
fellatio (sixty-nine); (7) performing sadomasochistic acts
(mild, not severe) upon a woman; (8) being masturbated
by a woman; (9) performing simple cunnilingus; (10) masturbation." The key words, you'll notice, are "a variety of
positions, or activities, changing from time to time." Show
this list to your lover and find out her particular ranking,
then work your way to the top. When you're done, vow not
to repeat any of the basics until you've tried every trick in
this book. Now is the time for a year of living sexually.

3. The Binaca Blast

Have you come across the Binaca Blast? It's something that every sex enthusiast should know about: Each partner places six to ten drops of concentrated Binaca breath freshener on the tongue before performing oral sex on his or her mate. The sensation is fantastic. What's more, you never have to worry about bad breath.
—S.O., Copenhagen, Denmark

4. Hot Wax

Some of my friends have been trying to organize an orgy. The suggested party games include the old Wesson Oil tag-team wrestling match. Everyone would grease up and go at one another. I confess that the image of gleaming bodies slithering against one another—women's hands running up thighs to grasp erect penises, men's hands sliding from crotch to breast—is my idea of a good evening. One of the guys suggested that such antics are out of date. He recently read about something called a hot-wax orgy, where they drip candle wax over one another's bodies. Each drop of wax is a touch of warmth—to be removed after several layers have built up. The accompanying images—erections that look like the necks of Chianti bottles, breasts that look like ice cream shop concoctions—are kinky, but I have reservations. Isn't the hot wax dangerous?

—S.M., Baltimore, Maryland.

Hold the candle high enough above the skin and the liquid wax will have time to cool off. On a blindfolded partner, the hot wax feels like an unexpected kiss. Test the candle on yourself first. Also, it helps to shave the area first—the point is temperature, not torture.

5. The Flying Philadelphian

Unfortunately, I attend school in Philadelphia. Never mind the jokes, the facts are bad enough. But to get to the point: What is a flying Philadelphia fuck? The phrase has become part of my vocabulary in the past year, but I don't know for sure what it refers to. Can you enlighten me?

—D.O., Philadelphia, Pennsylvania

Actually, it's a form of fellatio—a particularly gymnastic variety that's billed as the ultimate sexual experience, probably because it makes such a good story if you live to tell about it. The recipe includes a curtain rod (a very strong one, we would think) or chinning bar; a rocking chair, and a cooperative partner. Robert A. Wilson, author of Playboy's Book of Forbidden Words, *describes the subsequent action: "The woman sits on the rocking chair while the man, nude, stands upon its arms, holding on to the curtain rod with both hands. She fellates him by rocking herself back and forth and, at the crucial moment, he lifts his feet off the arms of the chair and hangs from the rod. Allegedly, because every muscle in his body is under maximum tension, his orgasmic spasms will be magnified most salubriously."*

6. Indian Wrestling

Recently, a young lady spent the night at my apartment. After a strenuous session of tantric lovemaking, we collapsed backward and untangled ourselves. Lying there head to feet reminded me of the good old days in summer camp—I challenged her to a bit of Indian wrestling. Once. Twice. On the third count, we locked legs. As I started to pull her over toward me, she reached out and grabbed my penis, which became erect almost immediately. Shouting, "Foul!" I grabbed her below the belt and discovered, to her delight, that she was equally vulnerable. We lay there for several minutes with our legs entwined, stroking each other lightly, getting very excited. We soon reached the point where our whole bodies ached to be involved. Not wanting to shift position, we began to suck on each other's toes, on the noninterlocked feet. (I know this sounds confusing, but imagine how it felt.) The climax was terrific, precipitated mainly by the oral sex on the toes. I'm freaked out; I had no idea that toes were sensitive. Have you ever heard of anything like this?

—T.M., Des Moines, Iowa

Yes, it's a favorite form of foreplay among politicians, although they usually go for the whole foot. Seriously, though, toe sucking is a popular sensory awareness exercise in encounter groups. It's a novel way for couples to get to know each other intimately; it also gets them turned around in the right direction.

7. Undressing

New lovers almost naturally savor a slow disrobing—after all, you see another person's body for the first time only once. Each piece of clothing removed imparts an erotic friction and a sense of release to the encounter. Consider a blouse edged across a collarbone, a dress bunched just below an expectant breast, the descent of a pair of Levi's down an inner thigh, or the moment a woman arches her back to allow the removal of an undergarment. Now take a cold shower. Bear in mind that later, an economy of expectation may dictate a sudden striptease with both partners overcoming the obstacles between themselves and what they know is about to happen. If you think it might be worth the expense, buy your girlfriend a light cotton dress and literally tear it off her body. It's like splitting firewood. Her nakedness is so immediate that it will certainly kindle your fires.

8. The Guided Tour

As we read through women's erotic literature, we have noticed an entirely novel approach to undressing. One of the themes running through Nancy Friday's collections of women's fantasies as well as in Gothic bodice-rippers is partial disrobing. Men throw women over their knees and lift skirts to expose rounded white bottoms. They then comment aloud about their discovery, their appreciation of this or that feature, to audiences of strangers. Yes, this is reducing a woman to a single part of her anatomy, but in her fantasy it's okay—hell, it's powerfully arousing—to be politically incorrect. Exposing just one breast is sometimes far more dramatic than total nakedness. Telling a woman that her pussy is beautiful—maybe turning a high-intensity light on the area—turns the body into a stage, or a work of art.

9. Total Sense

The sexual revolution was not the sole property of the counterculture. In 1973 Marabel Morgan gave American homemakers her vision of sexual freedom. *The Total Woman* offered old-fashioned wives assignments and "guaranteed-to-work Total Woman principles." Here are a few:

1. Be an atmosphere adjuster in the morning. Set the tone for love. Be pleasant to look at, be with, and talk to. Walk your husband to the car each morning and wave until he's out of sight.
2. Once this week call him at work an hour before quitting time, to say, "I wanted you to know that I just crave your body!" or some other appropriate tender term. Then take your bubble bath shortly before he comes home.
3. Thrill him at the front door in your costume. A frilly new nighty and heels will probably do the trick as a starter. Variety is the spice of life.
4. Be prepared mentally and physically for intercourse every night this week. Be sure your attitude matches your costume. Be the seducer, rather than the seducee.

10. The Ice Dildo

In Andrew Blake's X-rated classic *Obsessions*, two women attack an ice dildo. The scene is sizzling: The ice seems to represent strength, resistance, an obstacle to be overcome. It shows the basic physics of lust: Sex exists to convert solids to liquid. If you want to try this, be prepared for a shock. Ice actually can create a burning sensation, as the skin sends blood to warm the affected area. If you want to re-create this scene, try filling a test tube or small vase with water and leaving it in the freezer.

11. Touch Games

If you want to find out what women think is sexy, read women's magazines. Some are catalogs of sexual techniques. In 1972 Helen Gurley Brown published *Cosmopolitan's Love Book: A Guide to Ecstasy in Bed*. What turns on a Cosmo girl? Here's a sample:

Take hot sheets from the clothes dryer and wrap your naked self in them. Alternative: Place huge towels over radiator. When towels are hot, wrap them around you.

Put on a long nylon nightgown and wear it into the shower. Watch it stick to your skin as water pours over you. Shut your eyes, think about something physically provocative.

Naked, slip on your winter coat. Shut your eyes and concentrate on the feel of the coat lining, the weight of the coat upon your body; feel the delicate pricks from the millions of tiny hairs.

12. Piggyback

I become wildly turned on by prolonged strenuous exercise. For a woman, I have huge, exceptionally muscular legs. While I am working out with weights, particularly during a heavy workout, the longer I go and

the more I have to really grind it out, the more turned
on I become. My body is hot, the muscles are straining,
the sweat is flowing, and the passion is growing. The
guy I go with says making love to me is like making it
with a bucking bronco, because I am very active. Last
summer, he and I got back to my place one night and
got into a friendly tussle by the car. Quite by accident,
my boyfriend ended up with his arms across my
shoulders and his legs wrapped around my waist. I
decided to carry him up to my apartment. It was maybe
thirty yards, then up one flight of steps, which really
felt good, then to my door. I was very reluctantly about
to let him get off when—wonder of wonders—I felt him
big and solid and hard against my back. I was almost
afraid to ask, but when I did ask him if having me carry
him piggyback turned him on, he said it was fantastic
and a real turn-on for him. He said that the feel of my
strong body working under him was incredible. I let
him off, but only long enough for us to get our clothes
off; then, with no urging at all on my part, he got back
on and I carried him up and down the length of my
apartment until we were both so turned on, we almost
attacked each other. Fantastic.

—J.S., Ann Arbor, Michigan.

*Thanks. We're changing apartments soon and we need
someone to help us move. Er . . .*

13. Right-Nostril Sex?

A friend from California has told me a surefire way
to interest a woman in sex, a technique as old as India

and as new as the most modern research. He says that the right and left halves of the brain differ in mood control. The right side deals with spatial relations and the left side controls language and mathematical functions. Recent research has apparently determined that each half of the brain is also responsible for different emotional states. The right side is largely the source of negative feelings, including depression, critical attitudes, and anhedonia (resistance to experiencing pleasure), while the left side tends to generate positive feelings such as euphoria, sexual enjoyment, and the kind of healthy aggression displayed by enthusiastic athletes. Apparently, researchers have found that the two hemispheres alternate in their dominance of our bodies roughly every two hours. That means that the average person will be better at verbal tasks for two hours and then at spatial tasks for the next two hours. Low-key, high-key, low-key, high-key, every two hours. Now get this: Air flow through a person's right and left nostrils seems to affect the pattern of shifts in dominance from one hemisphere to the other. At any given moment, everyone is breathing more through one nostril than through the other. If you don't believe it, check your own nostrils for an entire day and you'll be convinced. Now, according to my friend, a researcher has found that when air flows through the right nostril, there is greater activity in the left hemisphere, and vice versa. And he has also found that breathing through the previously congested nostril can help stimulate the less active hemisphere. If you block the right nostril, the person breathes through the left nostril, and there is a relative increase in electroencephalogram activity in the right hemisphere. Now, here is the trick: If your date is moody or generally not in the upbeat, high-key attitude you want for sex, ask her to plug her left nostril for fifteen minutes. She can just stuff some cotton up it. Her mood will shift to the left, happy hemisphere and you're home free. What does the Playboy Advisor have to say about this?

—W.L., Gary, Indiana

Right. It amazes us that anyone from California is able to reproduce, let alone have a meaningful sex life. Your friend's theory is based on fact—a researcher did find the left brain/right brain phenomenon you describe—but the connection between airflow and sex has not been established. But look at it this way: If you can talk a woman into sitting with her finger up her nose for fifteen minutes, you shouldn't have any problem talking her into sex. And it's not clear that sex happens in just one hemisphere. If you are talking, that's a right-brain activity, right? Or if you are calculating how many strokes or how much dinner cost or how many days since her last period, that's math. We prefer the old-fashioned method—we expect sex to drive us out of our mind, not into just one hemisphere. And then we wait two hours, and want to do it again.

14. The Hum Job

My girlfriend and I have heard about a technique known as the hum job. It's a form of fellatio in which the girl puts her lips around her partner's testicles and hums the "Star-Spangled Banner." The male immediately comes to attention. We tried it and nothing happened, even though my girlfriend hummed every song she knows. Now she's worried that she did it wrong. Any hints?

—M.H., Madison, Wisconsin.

Since your girlfriend's a cappella effort didn't seem to work, she might try a little instrumental accompaniment with the lip, tongue, and two-hand quartet.

15. Gift-Wrapped

There's a letter in a recent Playboy Advisor from a couple complaining about lack of success with a technique known as the hum job. May I suggest a variation: the gift wrap. Have your girlfriend mold some aluminum foil around your testicles and, with her teeth lightly touching the foil, hum her favorite song. The metallic vibrations should produce the desired effect.

—A.V., San Diego, California

16. The Chinese Basket Trick

This technique captured the imagination of soldiers on R & R during the Vietnam War. Once you read about it, you may start looking for houses with exposed rafters or a sailboat with one of those chairs they use to hoist people up the mast. If you don't have access to a strong basket, a hammock will suffice. Here goes: Lovers suspend a basket from the ceiling of their bedroom with a block and tackle. After disrobing, the woman climbs into the basket and lowers herself until her genitals come into contact with her partner's. (By the way, the basket should have a hole in it.) Some couples have the man raise and lower the basket, while the woman plucks the ropes as if they were the strings of a harp; the vibrations can be delightful. Other lovers twist the ropes before the woman gets in; the gentle unwinding motion adds a new dimension to the phrase "getting turned on." If you don't happen to have beams in your room, try the Chinese picnic basket trick. Toss a block and tackle into a basket and find a secluded wood where the tree limbs are fairly thick. If you lack the upper-body strength to pull the ropes, run a cable out to the garage-door opener. Make sure your equipment is secure, and never raise your friend higher than you would like her to fall.

17. The Lyons Stagecoach

Over the years we've encountered sex tricks in the driest academic studies. Gershon Legman contributed the following eloquent description of enthusiastic sex in a work called *Oragenitalism*:

All the motions of her hips and torso that the woman can use in coital postures where she lies, kneels, stands or squats over the man can also be used when she is in the same position over the man for cunnilingus or the 69. In particular, the woman can use—and should make a real effort to try to learn, and learn well—the superb pelvic motion or mysterious gyration . . . La Diligence de Lyon (the Lyons Stagecoach) . . . a rapid and continuous forward and backward rolling motion of the kneeling woman's hips, similar to that known in horseback riding under the name of posting or "bronco-busting," where the rider's body sinks and rises rhythmically forward and backward to match the motions of the galloping or bucking horse.

18. The Ant Farm

On the other hand, anthropologist Ivan Block's description—which I copied from a long-lost textbook years ago—of sex in the society of the Ponape (a group of Micronesian islanders) is not our idea of a picnic:

Impotent old men are employed to lick the clitoris with their tongues or else irritate it by the sting of huge ants, so that gradually the organ of voluptuousness is made more susceptible. At coitus, too, the men, at the desire of the women, must use not only their tongue but also their teeth to produce a local stimulation of the female genitals.

Did they really use ants? I doubt it. And even with the shortage of time facing two-career couples, do you really need to hire someone to contribute to the voluptuousness of your partner? Still, there is something here: Try using your teeth—gently—the next time you have sex.

19. The Oral Sex Survey

The other night my lover mentioned that he had experienced great head only a few times in his life.

Mind you, he wasn't complaining about the quality of our lovemaking, it was just that there were one or two episodes that stuck out in his mind, if not his pants. How can I improve my technique? All of the sex manuals say that oral sex is okay, but none really go into detail. Can you give me any pointers?

—S.B., Seattle, Washington

We love questions like this; it gives us a chance to convene the Playboy Advisor Advanced Tutorial on Wondrous Sex and spend hours in the test bedrooms confirming our data. You might ask your boyfriend to review those peak encounters to see if he can find anything particular that distinguishes great head from the merely incredible. He might be able to define the secret ingredient, but you should be warned that a lot of the people with whom we talked said that when it comes to oral sex, not having to give directions was a blessing. Surprise is more important than suggestions, improvisation more pleasurable than obedience or duty. There were a few techniques that were oft cited: Men seem to recall with special fondness their partners who swallowed the ejaculate, who performed deep throat or some other special trick (adding hands or teeth, handcuffs, feathers, whipped cream). Women liked men who did not stop at the first orgasm, who bopped 'til they dropped. Both sexes seem to like oral sex when it is done for its own benefit and not as some halfhearted form of foreplay. It seems that timing is more important than technique, though. Where and when you perform oral sex will make more of an impression than the specific combination of saliva and sensation. Oral sex is to intercourse what guerrilla warfare is to trench warfare: It's best on the fly, hit and run. If any of you have a special technique or episode, why not drop us a letter?

20. May We Have the Envelope, Please?

This is in answer to the Advisor's request for letters concerning oral sex. I say examine the attitude, not the procedure. I've found that the best oral sex is just that —a form of expression in itself, not just another method of foreplay, though there's nothing wrong with that, either. The really remarkable episodes in my mind always involve aggressive, enthusiastic women who aren't at all self-conscious about expressing desire. What seems to make the difference is the enthusiasm and timing. A woman walked up to me in a saloon once and simply said, "I was just sitting over there wondering what it would be like to suck you off." You'd better believe the evening ended in great head. Of all the really good times, it's not the method that stands out, but the motive. For the purpose of suggesting ways of making it better for Miss S.B. and her lover, I can only bring out a few points, such as they are. First: Have some idea of what you're doing, so the poor guy doesn't have to direct the whole episode as if it were a scene from a movie. I'm all for the communication of likes and dislikes, but it detracts from the spontaneity if every step has to be requested. Open up and just enjoy yourself. He'll probably enjoy it, too. Also, it's quite endearing to the man when the woman swallows the ejaculate. Last, my suggestion is to pick some really surprising time and/or place. Unusual places and impromptu timing do the trick here, too. I seem to get more response from going slowly, almost as if I were seducing her, even if we may have been lovers for a long time. Rather than use oral sex as a prelude to intercourse, just keep going. Don't get so rhythmic your moves are predictable. Stagger the times and places you place your tongue. Bounce from clitoris to vagina in a random pattern and use her quickening breath as a guide to her likes. The biggie, though, seems to be, keep going. Go for an orgasm or spend the whole night trying. Go for two. Go for three; what the hell! If she's enjoying herself, save screwing for another time. You'll have a very happy lady with you right now, and that's pretty nice. Time for a little more independent study on my part.

—E.J., New York, New York

What was the address of that saloon?

21. Fingers

My girlfriend has this great oral sex technique that makes me climax within fifteen seconds to two minutes. Her approach is something like this: While she is sucking my penis, she uses her thumb and index finger in an up-and-down motion on the blood vessel that runs along its underside. Then she uses the same two fingers under the sac of my balls, with each finger manipulating a ball in the same up-and-down motion. It's dynamite: The motion is similar to milking and produces an intense orgasm that drains my sperm and leaves me moaning. I would like to know if you have any explanation for the success of this technique. I have not found too many women who can duplicate it.

—W.H.C., Mill Valley, California

The penis is more sensitive on the underside than on the top. (Doctors believe that this is related to the thinner ventral skin.) Others have suggested that orgasm does not completely empty the sperm reservoir—that the milking action can produce a second orgasm by pulling out the last few drops.

22. A Master Speaks

After reading your request for comments on the style of fellatio, I finally gathered enough courage to write (not that I think you will publish it). I agree with what you said about attitudes, since this plays as much of an important role as do true emotion and the openness of the couple involved. When you combine those qualities with a truly polished technique, you can't fail. It is very important to become fully aware of your partner's body. Know what he likes, where he likes it to be touched, kissed, caressed, squeezed, licked, and bitten. This is achieved by spending as much time as possible in bed together, just feeling each other in a lazy sort of way. After you feel confident that you know some of the things he likes, do them. I enjoy kissing the inside of his thighs first and moving upward to the groin. He likes me to trace a line with my tongue from his groin, under his balls to his back. When I tease the anal opening with my tongue, going in and out, then quickly move away, it drives him crazy. His deep inhalation and the tightening of his abdominal muscles make me know he really is enjoying it, so I enjoy it and want to continue. I enjoy running my tongue from the base of the penis to the tip on all sides, then teasing the head by making circular motions around the glans with my tongue tip. Then, when he least expects it, I dive down the full length of the shaft and suck like crazy, moving my head around and up and down, so that he gets two or three movements at once. By then I am so overflowing with my own juices I find that I like pulling his leg closest to me right up between my thighs and slowly hunching. He gets the message and moves his leg slowly back and forth while he reaches down and flicks my nipple and squeezes my breast. If I am between his legs, facing him, I can suck and massage his penis with my tongue in a way that, should I choose to, I can make him have an orgasm whether he's ready or not. (It's really hard to explain it: You just have to be there.) Then I swallow all his juices and reach for a drink while he recovers.

Another thing we have discovered is that if he enters me almost immediately afterward, which he often does because I am squirming so violently by then, he can have a second orgasm in a very short time, with no recovery period needed. I think it is partly because he recognizes my needs and wants to satisfy me, and partly because I keep my vaginal muscles in such good shape that I can create such a suction I can drain him dry. What I'm really trying to say is that successful fellatio or cunnilingus takes some homework.

—N.M., Milledgeville, Georgia

23. Hand to Mouth

Oral sex is a lot more pleasant than most women are led to believe—the look on a man's face while you suck his cock is one of the most beautiful sights in the world. To begin with, for me, starting off slowly is important: slow kisses or brushing my hair along a guy's belly, and then a little tongue around the tip of his cock. Using my hands (as you suggested) is always important, to give the man the feeling that his whole cock and balls are involved without doing "deep throat." As I begin to take more and more of his cock in my mouth, it gets easier and easier to enjoy for us both. I try to suck and use my tongue at the same time, concentrating with my tongue around the head. And all the time using my hand either to go up and down with my head or (for a little contrast) go up with my hand while going down with my head. When a man gets close to orgasm, he gets harder and the noises he makes say it all.

—K.A., Detroit, Michigan

24. Slow Hand

Over the past year, I've developed a masturbation technique with my boyfriend. First, I apply baby oil to the head of his penis—this prevents irritation and creates a different sensation from what he does for himself. Then I slowly stroke him with one hand— occasionally giving a slight twist or pinch for variety. My free hand traces his thighs, scrotum, or stomach muscles. (I can usually tell from the tension in the last when he is close to orgasm.) My boyfriend claims that the climaxes brought about by this technique differ from the orgasms brought about by normal intercourse —they are almost excruciatingly genital. Lately, he has consented to being tied down, so that he can thrash about in feigned helplessness as I continue to masturbate him to a second orgasm and fellate him to a third. After several of these marathons, he has told me that he felt he was going to have a heart attack. Am I hurting him by doing this?

—H.J., Cincinnati, Ohio

He may have been describing physical ecstasy rather than distress—he did wait until you had finished before saying anything, right?

25. Masked Ball

Recently, I saw a movie that presented a novel form of seduction. A guy met a girl in the park. Both were wearing masks. Not knowing who she was, and vice versa, they made wild passionate love, then departed without a word. The idea of such an encounter appeals to me. I can imagine the scene. A mere glance between complete strangers and we would get it on, weather permitting. I feel that by doing it with masks, I would have the freedom to make love the way I want. I would not let her facial expressions rule my actions. Could you tell me if this is a good idea?

—A.K., New York, New York

The editorial we is divided on this issue; we think it's a great idea, but it has to be put in perspective. The fantasy has its place, but not in public. The police have been known to take a dim view of people walking into Central Park wearing masks. Actually, masking is an ancient tradition. Eastern potentates often had their concubines and wives wear masks. The carnivals of Rio are occasions for cele-

brating impersonal sex. (There's a very powerful scene in the movie Henry and June *where the two meet and fuck in the streets.) It's every man making love to every woman. It strips the sex of telltale facial clues, but makes the eyes more expressive. Of course, some people get carried away. We read a description of an orgy where people came dressed as Henry Kissinger, Richard Nixon, Shirley Temple Black, and so forth. Check out a mask store when Halloween comes around.*

26. Ticklish Situation

Not long ago, I picked up a very lovely woman in a bar on New York's East Side. We seemed to get along very well, and it was unusually easy to convince her to leave with me. I was somewhat surprised when she suggested we return to her apartment. This elegant lady had me in bed with her before I knew what had happened, before I had a chance to make advances on my own. In a very sensuous manner, she began asking me to perform various sexual acts that would please her. I eagerly complied, only to have her smile sweetly and whisper that I wasn't doing it to her liking. Suddenly, without my realizing it, she had slipped what seemed to be homemade bonds made of satin around my wrists and ankles. (I thought she was simply nervously twisting the loose bedsheet around me.) Finding myself bound securely, I started to worry. She grinned and said, "You didn't do very well. For punishment, I'm going to torture you by tickling you with my long fingernails." Well, she had very long nails and proceeded to tickle me with them. For at least forty-five minutes. She literally put my squirming body into spasms, and much to my surprise, I reached an unbelievable orgasm.

—R.G., New York, New York

27. An Eyelid for an Eyelid?

Do you ever wonder if anthropologists are practical jokers? In *Simon's Book of World Sexual Records*, G. L. Simon describes the following:

After a goat was killed, its eyelids were removed together with the eyelashes. First they were put in quicklime to dry; then they were steamed in a bamboo basket for not less than twelve hours—this procedure was repeated several times. Once completed, the process yielded a sex aid that could be tied around the penis (jade stem) prior to coitus. The goat's eyelashes were supposed to give the woman a pleasant tickling sensation.

If you don't have access to a goat, you can buy French ticklers at any sex boutique—they are oddly shaped rubber devices that, when worn around the base of the penis, give some added stimulation to the clitoris. Or perhaps you could use an old feather boa to achieve the same effect.

28. Suds

Suds. Nothing turns me on like lots of suds in a bathtub big enough for two. I first experienced this treat in a massage parlor—since then, I've made use of king-sized bathtubs in the houses of rich friends. In a pinch, I will settle for an outdoor Jacuzzi, but when it gets right down to it, I prefer bathtubs. I'd like to introduce my latest girlfriend to liquid lovemaking. The problem is, how can I find a hotel with a giant-sized tub?

—F.J., New York, New York

Would you believe bridal magazines? Many honeymoon suites come equipped with the accessories necessary for a weekend of kinky sex—mirrored ceiling and walls, giant tubs, vibrating mattresses, round beds, videotape equipment, and so forth. It's a shame to waste such goodies on beginners. Check out the ads, then check in. Don't let your girlfriend see the magazines.

29. The Pickup

I love having sex in unusual places, especially if there is a chance of being caught! I've done all the typical ones, kitchen floor/table/countertop, while camping (beautiful view down from 10,000 feet), and on the beach. But I think my favorite would have to be the time I had sex in the cab of a pickup truck. It was strange, I must admit. I had had a fight with my lover, and we went for a ride to try and work it out. We wound up in the parking lot of a church on the mesa overlooking Albuquerque, New Mexico. There was a busy street running along the parking lot, with headlights from the cars driving by lighting up the seats of the truck. The view was gorgeous, though, the moon shining down on the Rio Grande and the lights of the city, so we stayed. Well, after much crying and talking, we started laughing, then touching. Before we realized what was even going on she had climbed into my lap and we were making gentle love. The headlights streaming by didn't faze us a bit, but the cramped quarters did. After a quick moment of joy, we laughed, got dressed, and went home to the bed to stretch out. I'll always remember that view.

—S.O., the Internet

30. The Pushup

I have found a refreshing orgasm for men. After foreplay and giving my woman an orgasm, I get on top like normal but in a pushup position with my legs tight and straight. Then I penetrate and start pumping with a rocking motion. Here's the trick: You keep this up until you reach orgasm, then after a few seconds, release your body and relax. You will feel a rush down your shaft like having a second orgasm.

—J.A.S., Livonia, Michigan

31. I Will Let You Breathe Through Me

A few summers ago I took a vacation with my girlfriend at my parents' summer house. We were skinny-dipping in the pool and soon enough things got hot. What we did was this. We swam over to the deep end, she sat submerged on one of the ladder rungs with her arms hooked around the railing for support. We then joined hands and she held me with my arms in a Y. I took a deep breath, she helped me under the water. Making an O with my mouth, I sealed myself to the lips of her vagina. I began performing cunnilingus. It took a few minutes to get used to the rhythm, but afterward I could stay underwater for ten to fifteen seconds at a time. She would sense when I needed air, pull me up, and then back to business. Afterward when we got out, she became very intimate. I thought it was because she came a lot. Later she explained to me that it was very symbolic for her, that I not only put myself in danger to please her, but that I showed absolute trust by letting her literally hold my life in her hands.

—D.C., Napanoch, New York

32. Ice Cream

In one of her books Dr. Ruth tells young girls that "Oral sex is perfectly natural and can be a great deal of fun. Pretend you are eating an ice cream cone." What kind of advice is that? Have you ever seen a girl eat an ice cream cone? They take a lick, wait a while, take another lick, wait a while. You get the picture. And when the ice cream gets really soft, they take a bite out of it. No thank you Dr. Ruth. You should correct your comrade.

—N.B., Sacramento, California

Actually, most of the women we know devour ice cream—by the quart. They let nothing stand in their way. We're getting hard just thinking about it. Dr. Ruth's advice was cute, but let's go it one better. Next time your girlfriend wants an ice cream cone, combine it with foreplay. While the ice cream is still in your mouth (or hers), perform a little oral sex. The cold can be quite a rush.

33. Ripe Mango

In the porn classic *The Opening of Misty Beethoven*, actress Terry Hall tries to give a lesson in cunnilingus to the title character. She suggests treating a woman's genitals as you would a ripe mango. The image of abundant juice, soft flesh, hunger is powerful—but the best part of the trick was the secret code. At one point in the orgy, she looks up and announces, "Ripe Mango: Take Two." Half of the power of the techniques in this book can be described as the bookmark effect. Name a sexual technique, and you can drop it in conversation with your partner—it's a discreet way of returning to the scene of sexual heat.

34. Grazing

Sex therapist Stella Resnick has explored ways of increasing our pleasure potential.

Get away from the notion that sex is an activity that lasts anywhere from 15 minutes to an hour and has a beginning, middle and an end. If you approach it that way you have a very short time to build excitement up from zero, and when it's over, you're back to zero again. Instead, encourage sex play daily, even for a few minutes. Let your desire build.

She calls it sexual grazing. You keep sex alive for a whole weekend, by walking up to your partner and giving her a hug, or a quick feel of the breast, or a kiss on the ear, then walk away. You find little niches to remind you of sex—rubbing back against a partner in an elevator. Remember making out in high school? They used to call it dry humping—moving your body in such a way as to tell your partner, "This is what I'd like to do." You keep the heat on simmer, then when you get into the bedroom, you are starting on warm.

35. In the Beginning Was the Butterfly

In an early episode of *L.A. Law*, one of the characters referred to a sex act called the Venus Butterfly. A polygamist with eleven wives had used the technique to keep his ladies happy. I have a suspicion that it has to do with the female labia, which, when spread, somewhat resemble butterfly wings. Can you explain the technique?

—T.S., Marysville, Ohio.

It's a new kind of Nielsen rating: Apparently, the producers of L.A. Law *were inundated with several hundred phone calls asking for more details about the Venus Butterfly. They got caught with their creative pants down. They took the official line that it was a secret technique and that viewers would have to watch later episodes. The response from the sex-starved hordes was such that it became a running gag. Since it didn't exist, the show's creators couldn't very well explain it; and according to our inside source (Deep Throat), they didn't even try (though executive producer Steven Bochco did give us baby oil in the microwave on* Hill Street Blues *years ago). The Venus Butterfly makes a marvelous Rorschach test. It brings to mind some of our favorite orchestral maneuvers in the dark.* The Sensuous Woman *had a butterfly flick, a fellatio technique that consisted of moving the tongue in circular motions about the male penis while sucking on it. Substitute the clitoris for the penis and you have something.* Xaviera's Supersex *mentioned the butterfly, a maneuver that involves flicking your eyelashes over lips, nipples, or other erogenous zones— slowly at first, then faster. The Pleasure Chest sells Joanie's Butterfly, a small vibrator that rests above the clitoris in a special G string. Clearly, none of these is ready for prime time TV. If the Venus Butterfly doesn't exist, it should. So we are announcing a contest: Invent a sexual technique that deserves to be called the Venus Butterfly, describe it in 200 words or less, and we will publish the best suggestions, after testing each one in the* Playboy *Test Bedrooms.*

36. The Ice Trick

One sex trick above all others belongs in this hall of fame. In 1961, at the height of the cold war, John Eichenlaub wrote a sturdy sex manual called *The Marriage Art*. In it he describes the following:

> Freezing cold against your skin stimulates both pain and temperature nerves, which are exactly the types of fiber which trigger sex climax. The ice-spurred special takes advantage of this fact. Before intercourse, the wife places at the bedside a bowl of crushed ice or a handful of cracked ice wrapped in a wet towel. Both partners strip and enjoy sex with the husband on top. As the husband starts his final surge to climax, the wife picks up a handful of crushed ice or the cold towel. Just as the paroxysms of orgasm start, she jams the ice cold poultice against her husband's crotch and keeps it there throughout his conclusion.

The movie version of *The Other Side of Midnight* depicted this technique. Of course, this raises the question of who sleeps on the wet spot—especially when the temperature is just above freezing.

37. On Pressing, Marking, or Scratching with the Nails

Sir Richard Burton first translated *The Kama Sutra of Vatsayana*, bringing the sexual wisdom of the Far East to the streets of London. The notion that every sexual gesture had meaning, that scratches could be used to create a dance of passion, still appeals. Consider this advice:

When love becomes intense, pressing with the nails or scratching the body with them is practiced, and it is done on the following occasions: on the first visit; at the time of setting out on a journey; on the return from a journey; at the time when an angry lover is reconciled; and lastly when the woman is intoxicated.

But pressing with the nails is not a usual thing except with those who are intensely passionate, i.e., full of passion. It is employed, together with biting, by those to whom the practice is agreeable.

Pressing with the nails is of the eight following kinds, according to the forms of the marks which are produced:

Sounding; Half moon; A circle; A line; A tiger's nail or claw; A peacock's foot; The jump of a hare; The leaf of a blue lotus.

The places that are to be pressed with the nails are as follows: the arm pit, the throat, the breasts, the lips, the jaghana or middle parts of the body, and the thighs. But Suvarnanabha is of opinion that when the impetuosity of passion is excessive, the places need not be considered.

38. The Butterfly Flick

There was a time in America when it was considered improper for a woman to possess knowledge about sex. That time was 1969, when an anonymous woman identified only as "J" penned *The Sensuous Woman* and gave us this trick:

One of the most arousing things you can do to a man is the Butterfly Flick. On the underside of the penis, about one to two inches behind the head, is a ridge called the corona. Just underneath the corona is a delicate vertical membrane. This is the most sensitive area of the man's body. To drive him straight to ecstasy, take your tongue and flick it lightly back and forth across this membrane—like you were strumming a banjo. Now run your tongue down to the base of the penis and back up again a few times and then return to the Butterfly Flick, only this time flicking all the way up and down the underside of the penis. Continue until the man begs for mercy.

39. The Venus Butterfly #1

Using temperature during lovemaking adds a new dimension to the variety of a couple's sex life. The method that strikes me as perhaps most similar to the *L.A. Law* scenario is to order hot water, crushed ice, and a couple of straws from room service. Place the hot water and the ice in two cups. After shooting the paper wrappers from the straws at each other (foreplay), put the cups on a small tray and place it on the bed. While your partner lies on her back, you perform oral sex using whatever pattern you prefer. Your only variation is that you make your lips and tongue very hot by sipping a little hot water through the straw. This can become even more exciting if you hold some of the hot water in your mouth and slurp on her labia. It sounds kind of funky, but what the heck. Although she probably will enjoy the hot water more, alternating with the ice will make the hot water seem even hotter (don't tell her which is coming next). Finally, if you put some mentholated tea in the hot water, it will drive her wild and help your sinuses at the same time. Bon appetit!

—E.D., Arlington, Virginia

40. The Venus Butterfly #2

The motel room overlooked the slowly flowing river, and my partner motioned toward the phone. I knew if I wanted it, I would have to make the call. I lifted the receiver and dialed room service. "Yes, I would like the peacock feathers out of the centerpiece in the main dining room, please. That's right, Room 969." As we awaited the familiar knock on the door, my partner and I exchanged baited glances and began to undress.

I took my position on the dresser, my bare back against the cold mirror, legs slightly bent and perched upon adjacent chairs. The anticipation was killing me. My nipples were growing hard and the tingling in my most sensitive place was beginning to hurt. The knock. The feathers arrived. My partner lowered the lights and walked toward me, tapping the flowing feathers against one hand like a sensuous riding crop. He began with my half-closed eyelids, working his way downward to my throat, then my breasts. Like the wings of a butterfly, the feather brushed against my skin, lighting only long enough to cause immense pleasure. It wouldn't be long now. The feather brushed down my torso and touched upon my most sensitive place, the most imperceptible fluttering, causing my body to shiver with desire. The dancing flicker provoked the fierce need for a hard tangible object inside me to complete our rendezvous. He gave without query.

—B.A., Austin, Texas

41. The Venus Butterfly #3

Pucker your lips, drawing them tightly around your teeth. Then, keeping the tension up, form a small opening the diameter of a pencil between them. Place your pucker on your partner's clitoris and move your tongue to the back of your mouth, forming a suction and drawing her in. Release the suction by moving your tongue forward again. This technique is distinguished from similar ones by the fact that the tongue is not used for direct stimulation, and with a little practice you can average between four and six reversals in direction per second.

—H.B., Holbrook, New York

42. The Trapped Butterfly

One reader submitted the following, from *Daiamyo's Revenge* by William Morell, as a possible clue to the Venus Butterfly mystery:

You will now learn about the Trapped Butterfly," he informed her. "I cup my hands on you so. Here, where you are most sensitive. I lower my face to my hands— so. My tongue becomes a butterfly trapped inside my hands. The way we did as children in a pleasant garden. Close your eyes, Diana-chan, and feel the butterfly trying to fly free, its fragile wings fluttering against your flesh."

Clenching her jaw to keep from crying out aloud and thus alarming any late working servants, Diana arched her back off the bed. When she could no longer stand it, she pulled him forward, over her, receiving him in a single thrust. Then the storm broke on the horsehair mattress.

43. Wanna Race?

Even books that parody sex manuals contain great tricks. In 1986, Tom Carey wrote *The Modern Guide to Sexual Etiquette for Proper Gentlemen and Ladies*, which gave us the following:

I think it's time we paid some attention to the manual stimulation of the male parts, as well as the female.

This can be a distasteful chore for many women at first, but like milking a cow, once you get the hang of it, it can be lots of fun. Make it a game. Hang targets on the wall. Try for new distance records. . . . Here's what I want you to do. Sit naked on your beds facing each other. Now, when I say go, I want you all to watch each other masturbate. Ready. Go. And no fair cheating. Girls, if you usually use a vibrator the size of a table leg, plug it in. Guys, if you normally drive carpet tacks into your nipples, then do that too. All good sex books recommend mutual masturbation. It'll help you better understand all the disgusting things your partner wants you to do.

44. How to Talk Dirty

My lover wants me to talk dirty to her in bed. I don't have the faintest clue as to what I should say. Can you offer any hints?

—T.S., Detroit, Michigan

Talking dirty can get you into the realm of the imagined and forbidden; it can be a great turn-on without being threatening. Here's a list of conversational icebreakers from an expert: If you're fucking in one position, tell her how much you'd like to get her in a different one. If you're in one orifice, tell her how you'd feel about being in a different one. Tell her how she'd feel. Tell her what she looks like with her pants down and her legs spread. Tell her how good she feels, how good she looks. Tell her you're going to tie her up—it's not necessary to do it, just tell her about it. Tell her you know how much she secretly wants to tie you up.

Tell her how good she is with her mouth or how good you're going to be with your mouth. Tell her you have fantasies about her in class, at the office, in the elevator. Tell her you are going to fuck her in class, at the office, that only you know what a sexual animal she is. Tell her that she's in control. Tell her to rub your cock with her pussy. Tell her her pussy's on fire . . . Get the idea? Shock value is erotic. Don't try to clean up your act; if you're going to talk dirty, talk dirty.

45. The Joy of Juice

I thought I had experienced everything in the erotic world until the night my twenty-two-year-old girlfriend came into my bedroom stark naked, holding three large oranges and a knife. She carved a hole in the end of the first one and allowed the juice to drip all over my genitals. She cut the second one into four wedges, squeezed them, and licked the juice off my scrotum. She then forced the head of my erect penis into the hole of the first orange, gently squeezing and turning the orange until I came. She halved the third orange and rubbed it all over her body, which I licked clean. Then she asked me to squirt the juice directly on her vagina. You take it from there.

—F.B., Hesperia, Michigan

46. The Chinese Basket Trick Blow Job

We saw a porno movie in which a man attached a pulley to a beam in the ceiling, then hung his girlfriend by the heels via a rope running through the aforementioned pulley. (Her hands were bound behind her back, but that touch is optional.) Lying on his back, he positioned the girl over his upright member and alternately twirled, raised, and lowered her until the blood rushed to her head, his head, and hallelujah.

47. The Swiss Army Fuck

Once women began to write erotica, our repertoire of what was permissible in bed increased dramatically. In *Herotica 3*, Mary Maxwell gave us this technique in a story called "Trust":

She reaches into a drawer in the bedside table, turning momentarily into the light. Her face is flushed, excited, her mouth a little open, her eyes bright. From the drawer, she takes a knife. The blade is as long as his hand, curved slightly, like an erect cock. "This knife," she says.

. . . He holds out his hand for the knife. She doesn't hand it to him; instead she grasps his wrist with her other hand, warm skin against his, and rests the blade lightly against his wrist.

"It's cold against your skin, isn't it? It takes your warmth away. It takes your breath away." She strokes his wrist with the flat of the blade. She stops stroking his wrist and slowly turns the blade so that the edge rests against his skin. "Even now, as long as you don't move it won't hurt you."

After a moment, she lifts the blade away and releases his wrist. The skin where the blade has rested tingles from the chill of the metal. His wrist is a study in heat and cold: hot where her hand had held him, cold where the blade had touched.

48. The Canteen

In the X-rated classic *Immortal Desires*, an army nurse tends an injured soldier in a bombed-out building. She offers him water from a canteen, then, taking a swig herself, begins to perform oral sex. She swirls the water in her mouth, letting the excess trickle over his body. She also pours water over his chest, and later, over her own body. The rivulets, if warm, become like long tongues of touch.

49. The Tale of the Tape

The other day I saw a videotape of a porn movie that showed the first new sex trick I've seen in years. At an orgy, the men took foot-long strips of adhesive tape and applied them to different parts of a woman's body: along the thigh and on either side of her breast. Then, as she approached orgasm, they pulled the tape off, causing her to writhe in ecstasy or pain or both. Probably the best thing about the scene was the suspense—you knew they were going to pull the tape off; you just didn't know when. I'd like to try it; but just to be on the safe side, is it dangerous?

—J.R., San Francisco, California

You survived childhood, didn't you? The trick is older than video—the cover of novelist John Nichol's first novel, The Sterile Cuckoo, *showed a woman covered in Band-Aids. As for the suspense, you left out one other crucial fact: whether to pull it off fast or slowly.*

50. The Savage Beast

The Kama Sutra came up with 529 sexual positions. Many are the result of mimicry. Lovers should couple like animals: "the congress of a dog, the congress of a goat, the congress of a deer, the forcible mounting of an ass, the congress of a cat, the jump of a tiger, the pressing of an elephant, the rubbing of a bear, the mounting of a horse . . . ," all the while making the appropriate sounds.

Start simply. Next time you make love, growl. Bite your partner's neck. Devour her.

We've come to view the sexual moment as a stage. You don't have to be yourself. You can tap into mythic creatures. There is a whole Native American sexology built on identifying with totemic animals—sex in the way of a bear, a deer. Why not go to bed with Bambi or Thumper? If you want to experience the effect of identifying with a wild beast, rent John Leslie's X-rated *Curse of the Cat Woman*. A black panther hunts in the night: the growl powers the sex that is happening in a rain-soaked alley.

Of course, why limit yourself to the animal kingdom? Why not make the sound of a Harley-Davidson?

51. Weightless

Gravity is the enemy of sex. The worst thing that ever happened to intercourse was the mattress. Let's go back to the forest. Make love standing up. Have a partner hang from a chin-up bar, with her legs wrapped around your waist. Find a jungle gym and entwine yourself in the bars. Find a swing or old tire hanging from a tree.

Suspend a platform bed from the ceiling by ropes. The man can stand on the floor, the woman can lie on the bed, offering either her mouth or her vagina. Let the slow swinging motion bring her into contact with your erection. If she can surrender to the pendulum, it will feel like she is being moved by a great force outside herself.

52. The Tent

Pitch a tent in your living room. Imagine you are outdoors. There is something primeval about lovemaking in a cocoon. The tent cuts off the outside world and creates an intimate space. Toss in a few pillows. Pretend. You are the last two people on earth.

The lovers in the Japanese film *In the Realm of the*

Senses spent weeks in a tiny room, and the bamboo and rice paper walls became a sexual universe.

There is a secret here: A lot of people try to make their apartments or bedrooms into a boudoir—but the elimination of distraction can also work. If you can still see your computer, you are not in the right place for sex.

53. The Flashlight

We'll get to candles later.

Take a flashlight with a narrow high-intensity beam. In an absolutely dark room, play the light across your lover's body. Let the light follow the path of your sexual gaze—what you see in your lover, what you dwell upon. You can add a soundtrack.

Think of the movies where the laser gunsight—the bright red dot—tracks across an unsuspecting target. This is the loving version of that.

54. The See-Through Shower

The Cliff Lodge at Snowbird, a ski resort in Utah, has rooms with see-through bathrooms. The architect wanted people sitting in the tub to be able to see the mountains, but the glass wall has another unexpected dividend. You can watch your lover shower. You get some useful information—how your lover touches his or her erogenous zones, what deserves extra attention. It is a form of foreplay that you cannot rush. See what makes your lover sing. You can do this at home with a see-through shower curtain, or at hotels with glass shower stalls. Of course, to make this work your partner has to forget she ever saw *Psycho*.

55. The Trim

I recently bought a hair clipper. One evening I took it into the bedroom and asked my wife if I could trim her pubic hair. She was all for it and had an orgasm soon after I began. I have been trimming her ever since and our sex life has improved. The thing is that my wife now wants to give me the same treatment. The problem is that I shower with other guys after work. How would I explain my clipped pubic hair?

—T.K., Detroit, Michigan

Trimming is less threatening than a complete shave with a razor. The vibration from clippers can induce an orgasm in and of itself. Plus trimming gives other benefits: the shorter the pubic hair, the bigger the organ. At least that's how it will appear to the guys at work, should they look.

56. The Close Shave

The previous trick is for beginners. After you've given each other a trim, go all the way. Pull out the shaving cream and razor. Erotic shaving defines empowerment (a word we always thought meant buying batteries for the vibrator). You are altering the look of your primary sexual feature—you are customizing your sexuality. It is a unique statement that has tactile benefits.

Men: Consider shaving the pubic hair from the shaft of your penis. Some women experience pain from deep penetration that brings them into contact with the short stubbies. When the woman is on top, that final inch along the bottom is what she rubs against—make it saddle-smooth. She'll appreciate it. We've found that it changes the way we experience the penis—it makes the skin more sensitive, and elongates what we think of as the primary erogenous zone.

Women: Consider leaving all the hair above the clitoris, removing all the hair below, and along the thighs. It extends the erogenous zone—connects the skin of the labia with the skin of the thighs.

57. Hollywood Sex Trick

A few months ago, my friend and I caught the movie *Personal Best*. Our question is this: How did Robert Towne persuade two totally heterosexual ladies to engage in a love scene? I've been trying to get women to do that for years. What was his secret?
—F.S., San Diego, California

In an interview with a film critic, director Towne gave his formula:

We prepared in a very special way for those scenes, using a lot of rehearsal and improvisation. And on the day we shot . . . the preparation was all physical. From six in the

morning until one in the afternoon, I had them both mas-
saged constantly to relax them. Then into the steam
room. Then into the whirlpool. Then back to the mas-
sage. I told the masseurs to stimulate them erotically, not
obviously. When they came onto the set, they were al-
most giddy. I had them sip half a glass of beer through a
straw to oxygenate the alcohol. They got giddier. During
the scene, which I encouraged them to play as loosely
and naturally as possible, I even played Boz Scaggs mu-
sic to them through tiny earphones. I think the scene feels
natural.

58. Deep Throat

When *Deep Throat* first came out, we consulted a professional sword swallower—who swallowed real swords
—for his tips. Here they are: "Throw your head back as
far as it will go. This opens up the throat and allows you
to accept an elongated object without gagging. Lying on
your back with your head over the edge of a bed is the
most comfortable way to maintain this position. Hold
your breath. (Impractical in this context; we suggest you
breathe through your nose. Linda Lovelace says she
breathes around the penis on the outstroke.) Practice
with a blunt object before you try the real thing."

59. The Alka-Seltzer Room Service Butterfly

After a satisfying dinner and a nice bottle of wine, already brought to us by room service, we relaxed on the sofa to some soft music. As I embraced her, she ran her fingers gently through my hair. Then she whispered, "Call room service for the Alka-Seltzer." She must have read my mind. I called instantly for the old *plop-plop-fizz-fizz*. Room service arrived with the little gems and my wife became quite aroused. We both knew what lay ahead and did not waste time. After we undressed each other, we engaged in some erotic kissing, licking and some heavy petting. Then she whispered in my ear, "Is it time?" I said, "Yes, it's time." I took an Alka-Seltzer, broke it in half, and inserted it into her wet pussy. It started to fizz, sending her body into helpless waves of ecstasy. I entered her and soon we both exploded in orgasm. Needless to say, we used up every bit of the remaining Alka-Seltzer.

—M.V., Akron, Ohio.

60. The Venus Flytrap

It involves a soft biting with a rapid flicking of the tongue over the bitten area, simultaneously and in succession. The biting is similar to the action of the Venus flytrap as it closes over a finger, and of course, Xaviera's butterfly flick can be applied to either sex with just a little imagination. I do not limit this technique to any particular erogenous zone; however, I prefer to start with the lips and tongue, moving to the earlobes and the nape of the neck, then down across the shoulders to a point beside the breast and the armpit, then to the underside of the breast and the nipple. I enjoy a little extra time feeling the nipples harden to my touch. Next I move to the abdomen, hips, buttocks, and thighs, moving down across the lower legs and back up again in reverse order before going down on what should be at this point a very hot, moist vagina. I have subsequently found that the lips of the labia and the clitoris are particularly sensitive and require intuition or a vocal partner, as the more aroused we both are, the more pressure I use. Also, I tend to alternate between biting, flicking, and kissing my hapless and ecstatic victims.

—D.H., Riverside, California

61. Cafe Olé

Here are two suggestions: When my lover performed the Venus Butterfly, he began by calling room service for a pot of coffee—strong and black. Everyone knows that coffee is the one true aphrodisiac. He would take a small sip of the hot coffee, making sure it was not too hot for the tender labia and clitoris, and then nip, lick, suck, and gargle the clit and surrounding skin until the coffee cooled. Then he'd repeat the process. I'm not sure if the secret is the heat, the caffeine, or the tongue action. But it is probably the length of time spent using a whole pot of coffee in this manner. Or my lover would phone room service for a napkin ring and a pair of chopsticks. He would proceed to place the napkin ring on his penis, in the manner of a cock ring (don't try this at home, kids). Taking a chopstick in each hand, he would roll the pubic hair on each side of the vagina into a tight curl around the stick and gently pull back the two lips. Then he would lick and screw as though there were no tomorrow. It's so simple.

—M.D., Novato, California

62. Symmetrical Sex

The female partner assumes a prone position, with her legs partly spread and her derriere just a bit elevated. Her skillful male partner then enters her vagina from behind. Simultaneously, he places the forefingers of each hand (for maximum effect both are required) at either side of the lady's clitoris. This biwinged approach resembles a butterfly. His hands help support her thighs, and as he thrusts into the vagina, he gently applies friction to each side of the clitoris, massaging in rhythm with his other movements. The gentle tugging lends additional pressure to the vaginal introitus, generating sensory overload.

—J.T., Northfield, New Jersey

63. The Blue Venus

For years I have been practicing this technique with great success, though it is the late great blues legend

Muddy Waters who should be given credit for inventing it. I learned of it by reading an interview with him published years ago. However, he did not give it a name. Take your penis (hard or soft) in hand and, starting at the south end of the vagina, gently rub the head into the groove of the vagina, lightly sliding it upward to the clitoris. Now reverse the process and slide slowly back down. Repeat. After a few gentle repetitions, the labia should begin to unfold, with the cleft moistening. If it wasn't hard when you began, the penis should begin to harden. Now you have prepared yourself and your partner for the Venus Butterfly. Gently work the shaft lengthwise into the fold of the vagina. This is when you achieve the likeness of a butterfly, with the shaft of the penis as its head and abdomen and the labia as its wings. What's more, even the smallest penis will adequately stimulate the largest vagina and the smallest vagina will comfortably accommodate the largest of penises.

—W.G., Kansas City, Missouri

64. The Movable Feast

First, order the following items from room service—roast duck, baked potatoes, a raw vegetable plate (with ranch dressing), steamed carrots, and two sticks of butter (wine optional). The meal must be brought up on a sterling silver cart. After the dinner is brought up, begin to feast; you will need your strength. When you're finished dining, unwrap one stick of butter and spread it on top of the cart (having first removed the dishes). Then place the cart close to a wall, directly across from the bed (you must be at least fifteen feet across from it). The male partner carefully gets on the cart, lying on his back, bending his knees to a forty-five-degree angle. He then slowly helps his lover on top of him. She gently moves from side to side; then when her partner reaches full penetration with his penis, she begins a slow up-and-down motion. Just before climax, the man will push off the wall with his feet, which will thrust the cart and the couple across the room (be sure to remove all obstacles in the way). When the cart hits the bed, the couple will slide off it and be launched into the air. During midflight, the male will pull down on his lover's waist and push his lower body forward. Simultaneously, his partner will lean back and pull on his shoulders while climaxing in midair, thus completing the Venus Butterfly. Note—the extra stick of butter is for round two.

—T.G., Bakersfield, California

We were going to say, "Now kids, don't try this at home," but who has room service carts at home anyway?

65. Wish You Were Here

A friend who has traveled in the Far East told me about a sexual experience he had with an Oriental woman that I originally found difficult to believe. He related that during their love play and the initial stages of intercourse, the young woman had gently inserted into his anal orifice a silken cord into which she had tied small knots. At the moment of climax, she removed the cord one knot at a time. To hear my friend tell it, it was the most unbelievable feeling he had ever had. If one wanted to try it, where would one get a silken cord that would be suitable for this type of activity?

—K.J., Huntsville, Texas

The technique goes by several names, from the Seven Knots to Heaven to the Briggs and Stratton Effect. (Pulling the cord resembles the act of starting a gas-powered outboard motor.) Any cord will do. Improvise: Some people use a string of pearls. Inmates at the Club Med used to lose a lot of beads this way.

66. Hot Air?

My girlfriend and I have a balloon fetish. We love making love on them. It started when we were messing around in the bedroom after a birthday party. When her back was turned, I decided to sit on a balloon to see her reaction when it popped. Well, it didn't, and when she saw what I was doing, she came over to help me by sitting on top of me while I was on it. When it still hadn't popped after a couple of tries, I had an idea. It was one of the most pleasurable times we've ever had, and we've been using balloons ever since. The thing we like about the things is that we can use them in just about any position we desire—the elevation is fantastic, they create an added bounce, and feel so nice and soft when we're sitting on them. They do have a tendency to pop every now and then, but that's really fun, too.

—D.C., Avon, Colorado

Anyone with kids knows that the rooms filled with tiny balls at Leaps and Bounds, Discovery Zone, or Mickey D's suggest nonparenting, or is that pre-parenting, alternatives. Fill the smallest room in your house with inflatables and dive in.

67. Let Your Fingers Do the Walking

My girlfriend has suggested that she needs more foreplay and more stroking during sex. She says that intercourse is not as exciting as masturbation, because it's less dexterous. She says that I should spend more time using my hands and shouldn't rely exclusively on my genitals. Can you give me any suggestions?

—K.A., Skokie, Illinois

Here's how to do it. Wet the tips of your first two fingers. Your saliva will do; hers would do better. Make gentle contact with the marvelous, slippery flesh at the front of her vagina. Don't probe it; don't press it. Just feel it and suppress your own sense of time and purpose. Listen for a response. This is better than biofeedback. If you're on the right track, adjust your touch to your partner's response and extend the territory. You're not looking for the clitoris—not yet. Move your fingers to the entrance of the vagina. Gently enter it so that just the pads of your fingertips are inside, no deeper for the moment. Let your fingertips do a little flutter kick right there—not a mechanical one, but a sensuous one. If it works, stay with it. A little more penetration may be in order; if it isn't, try a little less. If things go well, you're on your own, but improvisation is in order. Slip in a third wiggly finger. Check out the G spot—it's on the front wall of the vagina, about two finger joints in. Take your other hand and gently play with her clitoris while both of your fingers are inside her. Better, use your tongue. Or use your free hand to stroke her ass. Do not jump on her when you think she's ready. Stay with what's working five to ten minutes after you get the ready signal. If she tells you she has to have it, don't give it to her—not then. Tease. Have her add her hand to yours, to suggest rhythm and direction. Clip your fingernails first.

68. The J Spot

Sex researchers gave us a new erogenous zone—the G spot. Hundreds of people went looking for it with their lovers. Some found the Y spot: You touch it and your partner asks "Why are you doing that?" Lailan Young, author of *Love Around the World*, found something called the J spot:

Japanese men do not particularly enjoy kissing a woman's mouth and few are attracted to her bosom. The reason is quite simple: They prefer her secret spot, which enlightened foreign visitors (male) returning from Japan call the J or Japanese spot. Men also have a J spot but it is usually smaller. . . . The problem about locating the J spot is that its exact position varies according to the growth of hair in the target areas. The apparent hairline is apt to vary according to posture and whether the object of your attention is lying down or bending backward. . . . The first step is to raise the index finger of your right hand and quietly run it along the hairline, that is along the roots of the hairs. This is not easy. Return the finger to the very center of the hairline and lo! Exactly one inch below the center is the J spot.

Our response: The entire spine, not just the nape of the neck, is an erogenous zone. Start at the top and nibble, lick, chew, suck, and scratch your way down to the coccyx and back. For every yawn, stretch, or moan assign a letter of the alphabet.

69. Wake-Up Call

We both enjoyed sex, and when we did get together, we made the most of our opportunities—four times during the night and once the following morning (by then I was very pleasantly used up). We had a regular routine. The first time was light and easy—just to take the edge off our appetites, so that the second time, we could aim for an extended session. The third time was relaxed and playful, and the fourth time was our special invention. After the third time, we would go to sleep while my cock was inserted in her from behind as we lay on our sides. (After three good sessions of sex, we were totally relaxed and slept like babies. We did not toss and turn—and never once did we become uncoupled.) After two or three hours, something amazing happened. Our bodies would wake us up with intense sexual throbbing—they were so thoroughly united that we could not distinguish which of us was responsible for it. After enjoying the feeling for a while, we then would finish the job—and go to sleep for the rest of the night.

—D.M.N., Lawrence, Kansas

We found an explanation for this: The body goes through cycles during sleep, known as REM (for rapid eye movement). The male becomes erect, the female becomes aroused. The first phase usually happens ninety minutes after you fall asleep. You can try this without the earlier rounds. Just set the alarm clock.

70. Finger-Snapping Good Time

My lover calls it the six-pack. She reclines on her back and I straddle her belly, facing her feet, pinning her just firmly enough to prevent her from struggling away from my control. With the fingers of my left hand, I tease her lubricated clit; my right thumb I keep in her vagina and my right forefinger—also lubricated—goes snugly into her anus. As she grows more excited, I gently pinch and wiggle her perineum occasionally, using about as much pressure as one would need to lift a six-pack of beer. From time to time during our congress, I rise on my knees and scoot backward, dangle my genitals above her active mouth, and enjoy her kinetic tongue. When she achieves orgasm, I keep her pinned to the bed; her hands cannot reach around my body to prevent me from extending stimulation to the point of ecstasy. She says it feels better than anything should be allowed to feel. She keeps claiming she's going to do the same thing to me—accommodating our anatomical differences, of course—but she just can't bring herself to touch my anus. We both bathe thoroughly before and after. How can I change her mind?

—J.R., Houston, Texas

Beg.
Buy a box of latex gloves—you can find them at pharmacies and paint stores. Play doctor. Read the next trick.

71. War Story

While I was in the Philippine Islands during World War II, our LST put into a small harbor on Luzon. One of the native people related how two young sisters had perfected a technique of male sexual stimulation to the point where they could empty the glands. In some cases, it was said, as much as three fluid ounces of semen had been ejaculated. The technique consisted of one girl applying a fragrant cream to the penis and, through hand manipulation, arousing a full, hard erection. When she had reached that point, the second girl would enter the anus with a finger of her right hand, its rubber glove suitably lubricated. While the man lay on his side with legs slightly bent, the first girl would firmly stroke the penis and massage the testicles while the second girl proceeded to massage the prostate. Through physical signals from the male and everyone's perception of the intensity of arousal and climax, an ejaculation occurred at such a moment that the man did not know whether the stroking or the prostate massage had been the initiating factor. The ejaculation was a divine experience. The amount of expelled fluid felt massive. An intense feeling of pleasure and euphoria swept through the body. Afterward, one felt totally devastated.

—D.A.D., Santa Clara, California

72. I'll See That Orgasm and Raise You Ten

The letter from D.A.D. about wartime sex in Luzon triggered my own memory of the Philippines, also during World War II. The scenario went like this: Our gang of four would meet outside a particular bar. We couldn't enter until all were present. We would then proceed directly to a quite high table that had ample room underneath. Each man would be served by an individual girl, who had brought her knee pillow. After serving us, the girls disappeared under the table. As one might well imagine, the intrigue was building and building. Ten dollars from each man was in the pot, table center. The first man who smiled had to pay for the beer. His girl was awarded the pot of $40 for her expertise.

—C.S., San Diego, California

Don't you hate it when a sex scene leaves something to your imagination? What did the girls do exactly? Play cards? Tell jokes? But this letter was the inspiration for later advice. It doesn't have to be guys competing with guys. Imagine a scene in a hot tub or restaurant booth, where you challenge your partner to masturbate to orgasm. Stare each other down and see if you can climax without giving it away.

73. Save the Breast for Last

I would like a shot at telling how a man should go about making love to a big-breasted woman. If the woman is experienced—and most big-breasted women are, because men tend to choose them out of the field of possibilities—then you have the other men's way of dealing with her to overcome. Most men give a few kisses and jump for the breasts. The true answer is to leave them alone: Work on loving her back, her ankles, her kneecaps, her shoulders, her earlobes—anyplace but the breasts and never the nipples. Why? Because that area has been used and abused—let it rest. A woman likes the tender touch; when foreplay is into five play—when the inside of the thigh is warm to the touch—then the breast may be approached, tenderly, fingertips first, caressing, drawing lines from the outer edge of the breast toward the nipple. Don't touch the nipple yet. Never grip it like a joystick. Nibbling, kissing, sucking are fine, but leave the nipples alone. Finally, on seven or eight play, the nipples are touched and kissed and sucked.

—A.E.R., Youngstown, Arizona

74. Advanced Masturbation

I happen to believe that the male tit has considerable potential for sexual excitement. To test this, I devised a bulb that creates strong suction when placed over the nipple. For the past few weeks, I have been giving my nipples a workout several times a day. The suction is sufficiently strong that I can pull hard back and forth and the bulb will continue to hold the nipple in a strong grip. It may be partly my imagination, but I feel that my tits have developed a high degree of sensitivity to my manipulation. The nipples stay constantly erect, even when I'm not playing with them. Although I haven't had a chance to test it, I feel that a woman's manipulation just by hand would make me come. By mouth it would drive me wild. The other day I painted a woman's face on the bulb. After a minute or two I was so worked up that I climaxed.

—M.R., Detroit, Michigan

75. God Helps Those Who Help Themselves

My favorite ritual leading to intercourse involves my wife's performing fellatio on me while I work on my nipples. (While in my early teens I discovered that I could attain an immediate erection by pinching and fondling my nipples.) Rather than sending conflicting signals to my nervous system, this simultaneous stimulation increases the sensation in my cock and my breast. Several minutes of such dual action leaves me in a state of absolute ecstasy, and my arousal level is at a peak. If every unwilling male puts aside any macho hangup he has about this unmanly approach to sex, he will discover a wonderful erogenous zone above his belt.

—T.T., Dallas, Texas

76. The Frisbee Test

We would like your comments on the Frisbee test—if there is such a thing. While we were skinning it around the house, looking for something creative to do, I picked up a Frisbee and tossed it to my partner across the room. She retaliated, but the space was too confining for a continuation, so I playfully hooked the edge of the Frisbee on her generous nipple. It balanced for a split second and then slipped off. The idea intrigued us, so it was worth trying again. This time, however, after some manual stimulation, it worked like a charm! If there was a record to be set, she set it. The Frisbee hung in place until we went horizontal. Is this a first? Do you suppose the Frisbee test could symbolize the end of foreplay and the start of something big?

—R.G., Santa Monica, California

Or you could play quoits with a Hula Hoop.

77. The Amaretto Popsicle

I love giving head to my boyfriend, but for an added treat, I sometimes pour Amaretto into a small brandy snifter. I sip it while we talk. As we get down to business, I dip my fingertips into the Amaretto and drip it onto his nipples and lick it off. I do the same thing to his cock. Often, he puts his fingers into the glass and I alternate between sucking his fingers and sucking his cock. I call him my Amaretto Popsicle. It certainly is fun.

—B.C., Troy, New York

78. Babes in the Hood

Here's my problem: When I begin to make love or perform oral sex, the clitoris is usually easy to find. However, when I look up to catch my breath, I try to see if it's still in view. Inevitably it is no longer in sight, and it takes me a minute or two to find it again. Is it just me, or have other guys experienced that kind of hide and seek?

—J.R., Memphis, Tennessee

Relax. As a woman approaches orgasm, the clitoris retracts under a hood of skin. Why it chooses that moment to play coy and hard to get is beyond us. However, the best advice is to keep on doing what you've been doing. The woman is close to orgasm, and if you interrupt the motion or the rhythm to find your place, she will lose her place. Our guess is that the clitoris hides itself in self-defense. There is a narrow line between stimulation and irritation. You may want to ask your partner to masturbate in front of you. See how she treats her clitoris; is the stimulation direct or indirect? Every woman is different.

79. Shower Power

Have you ever taken a shower with an exciting person in the dark? I have found that the proper music, wine, and lack of lighting in the shower are an absolute turn-on. Sometimes, depending on how you feel, very slight lighting is much better. Moonlight, for example, presents just the right amount of shadows and glimpses to excite me to the point of no return.

—B.W., New York, New York

We found that this trick worked wonders. Our date wasn't turned off by the ring around the bathtub, and we had a meaningful encounter with the shower curtain.

80. Pumping Pleasure

In high school, they placed a bar in a doorway (this was during gym session) and asked us girls to do chin-ups. I am very athletic, but I never made it. I didn't realize it then, but after just a few chin-ups I experienced an orgasm. Before I married, I discovered that if I hung on a door and tried a few chin-ups, I could—and still can—experience an orgasm in a matter of just five to ten seconds. Yet orgasm with a man is hard to achieve. Can you explain this phenomenon to me? Should I let my husband know?

—E.D., St. Louis, Missouri

You wouldn't be the blonde in the purple leotard at our workout class, would you? Never mind. Here's how to make your husband understand. First, remove all of his clothes. Stimulate him in whatever fashion you prefer, and when he is erect have him stand directly under the bar. Do a few chin-ups. Let gravity do its work. Try for a one-point landing. He'll understand. He may think it's weird, but he will understand. We have to ask why have you chosen to keep this a secret. The reason orgasm with a man is difficult is that you don't share what works. It could take him years to stumble upon the chin-up trick himself.

81. The Penis as Paintbrush

Women are always complaining that intercourse does not give the clitoris enough stimulation. They insist that men use their fingers to masturbate it. Why hasn't anyone suggested the obvious, that instead of inserting the penis, the man use it to stimulate the clitoris directly, holding it in his hand? What do you think?
—R.F., Cambridge, Massachusetts

Edgar Gregersen, the author of Sexual Practices, *describes a similar activity in two Oceanic tribes:*

The Trukese . . . call their coital technique wechewechen chuuk, "Trukese striking." The man sits on the ground with his legs wide-open and stretched out in front of him. The woman faces him, kneeling. The man places the head of his penis just inside the opening of her vagina. He does not really insert it but moves his penis up and down with his hand in order to stimulate her clitoris. As the couple approach climax, the man draws the woman toward him and finally completes the insertion of his pe-

nis. Before climax, as the partners become more and more excited, the woman may poke a finger into the man's ear. . . . The Yapese variant called gichigich *[goes like this]: The man just barely inserts his penis between the woman's outer sexual lips as she sits on his lap. The head of the penis is moved up, down and sideways for a period of time, which can be quite long. The rate of this movement varies and can become . . . intricately contrapuntal. All this is said to make the woman frenzied, weak and helpless. . . . Coincidence I think accounts for the fact that the Yapese, with this rather strenuous, frenetic sexual technique have one of the lowest rates of frequency for intercourse found in the world.*

82. The Paintbrush as Penis

Take an artist's paintbrush—preferably soft, although a different effect can be achieved using stiff bristles. Stroke it gently against your partner's clitoris or nipples. Draw long lines down the curve of her body. You can use a dry brush, or one that has been dipped in warm water or heated oil. Or, if you want to pretend you're at Woodstock, you can use water-soluble paints.

83. Angora Anguish

About a year ago, my girlfriend was wearing an angora sweater. It was very soft to the touch and feminine-looking. That night, while initiating foreplay, I slid my penis up under her sweater to get between her tits. I immediately noticed ultimate stimulation, as if the hairs in the sweater were tickling every nerve ending in my penis. She grabbed it and began to massage it. I was in ecstasy and soon came, and she swallowed it all. Then we made love—the best I ever had. She sometimes masturbates me with angora sweaters, as she knows how much I like it. I've noticed that the softer ones, with 50 percent rabbit hair and 50 percent lamb's wool, feel the best. I thought some of your female readers might want to try this on their mates. It sure drives me wild; it seems to get me up no matter how many times I've already come.

—C.B., Walnut Creek, California

84. Female Orgasm Self-Taught

In regard to your request for information on how orgasm was achieved or was learned, I have discovered a successful method that never fails me. When my man gets one of those unexpected erections that take him less time than for me to intensify my own clitoral erective stimulus, I first look at it and think of the heat and the power emanating from it, from the head right down to the shaft; then I concentrate on the other dominant masculinities, such as the hair on his chest, the hardness of his thighs, the testicles, where that sweet sperm is waiting or the desire in his eyes—in other words, the whole man! I envision and acknowledge his strength superseding my own. In that I find admiration and my first feelings of queasy vulnerability. I then feel him begin to mount me; I put my hands on his rib cage to feel the muscles and the heaving of his body and feel my love for him enter my heart. I close my eyes, place a hand on each buttock, and gently spread them while he is inside me (this makes me feel as if I am beginning to take control of his body and also he is able to thrust deeper within me). This is when I think of myself in terms of pulsation—the vulva, labia, vagina, and clitoris. I squeeze my vagina tightly, with the thought of resistance to him; that tightens pressure on his penis. At this point I envision myself winning the victory of resisting him with the strength in my vaginal walls, and picture my vagina drinking his warm semen; then I elevate my hips slightly to receive him and slowly pull my pelvis in a downward motion, as though I were nursing the head of his cock with a vaginal sucking motion, with the thought of tasting his sperm with my pussy. As I feel the heat rise, mine does also, and the victory is almost always a mutual explosion of orgasm. The formula: observation, respect, admiration, fear, battle, love, compromise, victory. . . . I have discovered through experience that if a woman suffers from insecurity, it can inhibit orgasm. Once you find your self-esteem as a loving, sensuous, responsive, and honest woman, you will see and feel those closed, stubborn doors opening up for you. You will also feel that the orgasm you receive is a gift bestowed rather than one received. In other words you excite me, I want you, I feel for you, I give you me, wrapped in the wetness of my feelings, surrounded by the warmth of my vagina to enfold your sperm into my safekeeping. And your man's orgasm is also a gift bestowed rather than a gift received.

—S.L.W., Lake Worth, Florida

85. More Orgasm Tips

I used to climax only with oral or digital stimulation until my husband brought home a vibrator. We just tucked it over my mons pubis during intercourse and I climaxed easily. Next we tried it with the vibrator on, but just set it on the bed, not on me, and had intercourse. I was able to climax—sort of a conditioned response. For some reason, just knowing I was capable of it made it easier the next time. But I can't have my first orgasm this way; I have to get things warmed up the old way first.

—G.B., San Pedro, California

86. Squeeze Play

I'm in my mid-twenties, am healthy, and have been dating my boyfriend for one and a half years. I have never been able to have an orgasm with him or anyone else through sexual intercourse but have always been able to have one through oral sex or masturbation. One time instead of spreading my legs (as most women probably do), I kept them as close together as possible, with my boyfriend doing the same while on top of me. In that very common, simple position, I was able to have an orgasm and have been having them ever since. They are getting longer and better now. I don't know if this will work for other women, but it works for me.

—R.E., Omaha, Nebraska

87. Lounge Lust

One day, relaxing on the bed during the afternoon, I felt the need to be closer to my husband—closer than just nestling in his arms—and draped my body over his. That was fine, but still did not bring about the closeness I was seeking; he raised his hips and entered me and we lay in that position for some time, neither moving. After a while I instinctively arched my pubis down to his and felt a delicious sensation that called for relaxing and repeated nudgings; then, with a slight side-to-side movement that felt too good to stop, I continued that grinding of my pubis against his, slowly speeding up the rhythm and the amount of pressure I exerted. All of a sudden, I felt an incredible wave of sensation that could only be the one thing I thought I'd never feel: the big O. The advice I have to offer is that nothing comes to those who wait. Go for it.

—T.H., Orlando, Florida

88. Supersize

We had been playing poker with friends until after midnight. Vodka had flowed abundantly and we were all relaxed and in an excellent mood. After our friends left, my wife went to take a shower, while I headed straight to the bedroom and undressed. I was about ready to dive under the covers when I spotted a bunch of bright red oval stickers on my wife's dresser. They read SUPERSIZE in big letters, probably some advertising for an economy pack of laundry detergent. I spontaneously decided to alter the purpose of the advertising to my benefit. I wrapped one of the stickers around my cock and checked the effect in the mirror. I burst into laughter at the sight of my glossily wrapped supersize. I was still posing when my wife walked in. She started giggling. The hilarity subsided somewhat when we tried to get the thing off. The glue on the back of the sticker proved to be very strong, and part of it had gotten stuck in my pubic hair. My wife knelt in front of me and tried to pull the sticker off as gently as possible. It hurt, tickled, and aroused me at the same time, and my cock grew, slowly rising to its horizontal position. The glossy red sticker had become a painful corset for my erect penis, and the fact that my wife was tantalizing its tip with her tongue, giggling endlessly, did not help my lustful agony. Finally, she grabbed the sticker at one end and tore it off with one vigorous pull, making me gasp from the sudden sharp pain. However, the pain gave way to intense lust as my wife started sucking passionately on my tortured supersize. When she pushed me gently backward onto our bed, my spontaneous advertising campaign was already very close to its orgasmic end.

—T.M., Long Beach, California

89. Putting on a Condom

So that putting on a condom is less distracting, my partner places it on me, which is very arousing for both of us. First she lubricates my penis with her saliva so that when I am thrusting, I am less aware of wearing the condom. After coming, I like to stay in for a while, assuming the semen will be contained safely in the reservoir end. If I stay in and work up to a second climax, the sensation of thrusting in my own warm semen is close to the natural feeling of the vagina.

—B.P., Washington, D.C.

90. Vibrator Tips for Men

Our favorite sex shop in America is Good Vibrations in San Francisco. Their specialty? Vibrators. In their anniversary catalog the store staff shared their collective wisdom with customers, most of whom are women, but some of whom are men. That's right. Men use vibrators, too. Here's how:

If applying a vibrator directly to your genitals results in a neutral or slightly unpleasant sensation, try holding your penis with your hand while pressing the vibrator against your fingers. Or start out using it through your clothing or a folded towel. Later as you become accustomed to the feeling you may want to apply the vibrator directly. Some men can be stimulated or stimulate themselves to orgasm with a vibrator; others become highly aroused with the vibrator, then switch to another form of stimulation if they wish to continue to orgasm.

91. Good Vibrations for Women

Most people mistakenly assume that vibrators are for masturbation only—and that one is enough. Sorting the catalogs from Good Vibrations or reading *The Good Vibrations Guide to Sex* by Cathy Winks and Anne Semans, one sees that there are many types of vibrators, and an almost unlimited potential for play. Suggestions range from using more than one vibrator (one per nipple, or front and rear) to using two-headed monsters (either for simultaneous vaginal and anal stimulation or to trap a penis between the two heads). If you inherited a Swedish-style massager (the kind you wear on the back of your hand) from your parents, turn it on and touch your clitoris, or run two fingers up and down your partner's penis. And more than one expert suggests using the vibrator as a means of exploring other erogenous zones, or unusual positions. Do it standing up, doggy fashion, or crouched over a magazine cover of Brad Pitt. Put a mirror on the floor and watch yourself. The possibilities are endless.

92. Sexual Shopping

My wife and I have never been to New York City and so have never seen the inside of a sex shop. But we have discovered catalogs. Our favorites are from Good Vibrations and Romantacy (two California sex boutiques), but we've also gone window-shopping in catalogs for Evelyn Rainbird and Adam & Eve. We've discovered that just looking is a turn-on. We see a blurb for a nipple clip or a clit clip and imagine ourselves using them. If someone has gone to the trouble to design something that pinches one's nipples just so for hours on end, then what do fingers feel like, if I grab my wife from behind and tweak her nipples just so for—well, not hours, but minutes on end. The clit clip, a device that encircles the clitoris and sort of holds it like a bunch of flowers, taught me to appreciate the shape of my wife's most sensitive area. I treated it like a tiny penis, running my fingers up and down the sides . . . you can imagine what happened next. And we discovered that for almost every device being sold, there is a sex aid cleverly disguised as a household item. Want a feather? Pluck one from a feather duster. Want a mask? Raid the kid's dress-up drawer. You don't have to spend money, but inevitably you may want to try the real thing.

—N.B., Boston, Massachusetts

93. Fire the Booster Rocket, Flash

We once saw a porn actress use a vibrator equipped with a sleeve—a tiny tip that she inserted into her anus. She did not turn on the vibrator until she was in the throes of orgasm; when she flipped the switch the second wave of sensation put her right over the top. You can hold a vibrator poised just above your partner's clitoris during oral sex or carnal touching—adding the crescendo or taking it away for delirious effect.

94. Hi-Ho, Silver, Away

An old girlfriend once told me that her favorite sex scene was in a book on the Borgia family by Marcus Van Heller, that for years she fantasized and masturbated to a scene where a woman was taken from behind—on horseback. While I'd like to fulfill her fantasy, this one seems out of reach. Any suggestions?

—J.P., Chicago, Illinois

We've heard of this being done: It takes a cooperative woman with great equestrian skills, not to mention a cooperative horse. (Horses symbolize wildness and all that, but sex can be difficult with only two separate intelligent entities involved—let alone that of a different species.) Besides, we've never met a horsewoman who let a man get between her and her horse. Still, the basic premise, coupling and letting another power supply the rhythm, can be used with other vehicles. Try one of the quarter rides outside a shopping center after hours. Or do this on a motorcycle: Find a secluded country road or large parking lot. Put your partner in front, wearing a short skirt. Enter her from behind—or if she is descended from the bull riders of Crete, she can lie with her back on the gas tank and her legs wrapped around your waist. (We have a picture of the editor of Bike *magazine performing this maneuver at 60 mph.) But you may want to try something less suicidal. Finally, for stay-at-home types, have your partner straddle the back of a sofa. Enter, and she can enjoy the pressure from both sides now.*

95. Dream Catcher

I know the Venus Butterfly was supposed to be something that the man did to the woman, but here is a technique that my husband and I discovered that at least deserves a mention. I woke up one morning before him and started to stroke his penis. I didn't grip the shaft, but rather ran the backs of my fingers up and down lightly, the way one plays with a strand of hair. He became erect and started thrusting—I let his penis slide between my fingers, across the back of my hand, never offering complete resistance. After a few minutes he said, "If you touch my balls with your other hand I will come." I did, and he did. He later told me that he felt his erection was trapped in some kind of sea grass or net—that it was unlike any kind of touch he'd ever experienced.

—S.T., Chicago, Illinois

96. Buñuel's Box

In Luis Buñuel's movie *Belle de Jour*, Catherine Deneuve plays a woman living out her fantasies as a prostitute. One of her clients is a large Oriental gentleman who carries a wooden box. It's about twice the size of a cigar box, and a loud buzzing, like the sound of insects, comes from it. I've always wondered what's in the box. How is it supposed to have been used during their liaison?

—J.E.H., Fairfax, Virginia

The mystery box in Belle de Jour *is the counterculture's equivalent to* L.A. Law's *Venus Butterfly. Does the box contain a hive of hungry bees or love-starved beetles? One of the prototypes of the Orgasmatron vibrator? Angry dentures that you could wind up and turn loose on your lover's body? Buñuel, in his autobiography,* My Last Sigh, *complains, "Of all the senseless questions asked about this movie, one of the most frequent concerns the little box that an Oriental client brings with him to the brothel. He opens it and shows it to the girls, but we never see what's inside. The prostitutes back away with cries of horror, except for Severine, who's rather intrigued. I can't count the number of times people (particularly women) have asked me what was in the box; but since I myself have no idea, I usually reply, 'Whatever you want there to be.' "*

Do any of you keep toys in an erotic hope chest? Tell us what's in your tool kit and we'll publish the best.

97. Room Service Sex: Take Three

The Venus Butterfly scenario required a call for room service. Most hotels offer traveler's kits with toothbrushes, mouthwash, a disposable razor, shaving cream. Call down and ask the front desk to send one up. Then use the toothbrush to lightly stroke the skin around your partner's nipple. Alternate the brush with the hard side; use the entire thing as a tiny paddle. It works on male anatomy as well. Your partner can use the mouthwash during fellatio to swirl around (alcohol may be too painful on the clitoris). And as for shaving . . .

—L.D., Boston, Massachusetts

98. When Naughty Is Nice

I'm still shaking. The other evening, in the middle of sex, my girlfriend looked me directly in the eyes and asked me to begin spanking her. My first reaction was to laugh, but I could tell from her look that she was dead serious. So I spanked her—tentatively at first, then with an enthusiasm that took me entirely by surprise. I was inside her at the time and the physical reaction she had—squirming, then damn near bucking —made the intercourse much more pleasurable. The two of us came like never before, and I can honestly say it was the best sex we ever had. But what worries me is, why did we both get turned on by something so, well, kinky?

—R.G., Baltimore, Maryland

For most of us, spanking is one of those little sexual demons inside us that always takes us by surprise when they surface. After all, we're not in bed for the purpose of pain, so anything that even smacks of it is going to be foreign to us. So we asked a lady friend to describe the turn-on: "For me, spanking is a very distinct, two-headed beast. Emotionally, it's the concept that I am being entirely controlled— consumed, dominated, then conquered. Then there's the actual feel of it: being entered on one side and paddled on the other. I simply lose control."

98. Joystick

Here's a sexual pick-me-up that my wife and I have discovered puts a little zap! boom! bang! into our love life. We bought a fast-paced computer game, then set it up on our home computer on the kitchen table and sat together facing the screen. My wife sits between my legs. We share a joystick and take turns jumping rocks or holes with the speeding moon patrol vehicle. As each of us takes control of the joystick, the other provides distractions, such as kissing, touching, blowing. The only hard and fast rule is that neither of us can leave our sitting position or interfere with the partner's joystick hand. After each game, the low scorer discards a piece of clothing and we play again. It is an incredible turn-on to see my wife's hand wrapped around that wiggling joystick as she struggles for control and I kiss her neck and fondle her breasts and pussy. Eventually one of us is disrobed and we end up making love in the chair or on the floor.

—B.C., Bakersfield, California

100. Afterglow

After we both come, my wife and I like to hold each other and feel close and kiss and talk and fool around. We'd like to linger in afterglow even longer. Any suggestions?

—B.R., St. Louis, Missouri

In Romantic Interludes: A Sensuous Lover's Guide, *Kenneth Ray Stubbs and Louise-Andrée Saulnier recommend extending afterglow by taking turns giving each other facial massages. The massager sits up, legs apart. The massagee lies between the other's legs on his or her back. Using light to moderate strokes, the massager starts at the top of the head and works down across the forehead, along the bridge of the nose, across the lips, and down to the hollow under the chin. Then the massager caresses the jaw and works up across the cheeks and temples, finishing with the ears. "For a final touch," Stubbs and Saulnier write, "cup your palms around [your lover's] ears. Closing off external sounds brings your lover to a womblike world of breathing and heartbeat. For some this can be a mystical experience." After a few sessions, we became convinced that afterglow was a misnomer. Now we call it encoreplay.*

101. Candid Camera

For Christmas, my wife of two years gave me a video camera and a tripod. I used the camera regularly for a while, then lost interest. Then one night when I came home, she sat me down in front of the TV, popped a tape into the VCR, and cuddled up next to me on the couch. To my absolute astonishment, the video showed my wife wearing lingerie and puttering around in the kitchen. Then she undressed slowly, climbed onto the table, and began masturbating with her legs open to the camera. At that point, I begged her to make love to me. Watching her on the screen at the same time we were having sex was the most erotic experience of my life.

—C.N., Nashua, New Hampshire

102. Latex Lifesaver

Are there flavored condoms? I sometimes want to perform safe oral sex on a partner, but the taste of latex is a bit much. Any suggestions?

—J.G.S., Savannah, Georgia

Try sucking something else at the same time—a mint Life Saver will do nicely. The mint flavor makes condoms more palatable, and some men say that the combination of a soft tongue and a hard Life Saver provides some extra stimulation. Sources very close to us recommend wintergreen, but experiment for yourself.

103. How to Perform a Striptease

When my boyfriend's brother got married recently, one of his friends arranged for a stripper to entertain at the stag party. The young lady who performed started out in a police uniform on a ruse that the guest of honor was being arrested for unpaid parking tickets. Then she produced a boom box, turned on some raucous music, and started peeling—and playing imaginative games with her nightstick. The stripper's performance made a big impression on my boyfriend. He has always liked my body, and sometimes I show it off by going around the house braless in a thin top or without panties in a short skirt. He always gets turned on, but the reactions I've elicited don't hold a candle—or a nightstick—to the excitement the stripper created. Our anniversary is coming up, and for his gift, I've decided to perform a striptease dance. Got any suggestions for a truly memorable celebration?

—T.D., Indianapolis, Indiana

We sure do, courtesy of our old friend Fanny Fatale, for seven years a professional stripper who has raised men's blood pressure—and other things—at erotic showplaces all over the country. First of all, don't think of stripping as dancing. "Stripping involves dancelike movements," Fanny says, "but that's only part of it. Real stripping involves creating your own sexual fantasy and living it. The more you live your fantasy and get turned on yourself, the less embarrassment you'll feel as you peel, and the more your man will love it." So, what's your fantasy? Naughty nurse in a white uniform? Corporate executive in a power suit? Socialite in an evening gown? Fresh-faced coed in cheerleader gear? Whatever you choose, see your outer garments not as clothing, but as costume, and splurge. "Overdo it," Fanny advises. "Sleaze out. Use props. Pile on the costume jewelry. Tease your hair. Wear garish lipstick. Sometimes all it takes to get the effect you want is big hair, big lips, and very high heels." Under your costume, deck yourself out in the lingerie you've always dreamed of. The one piece that's de rigueur is a G-string. The steamy strip's final ingredient is music, ideally rock or rhythm and blues. Pick three favorite songs that have lusty beats. They should be easy to dance to, and the beat will provide inspiration that helps you live your fantasy. "For best pacing," Fanny says, "choose two fast songs and one slow one." During the first song, discard your props and slowly take off your coat, hat, gloves, and dress. During the second, slowly remove your nylons, garter belt, and bra. And during song number three, retain the high heels, but say good-bye to the G-string. "Once you're naked, do some floor work," Fanny advises. "Get down on your hands and knees and roll around like a cat. Crawl up to your guy. Drape yourself over him. Take off his belt. Unbutton his shirt." We figure you can take it from there.

104. Freeway Fellatio

Since my husband has never liked my family, getting him to accompany me on visits used to be hell. Fortunately, my husband's in-law aversion recently changed to enthusiasm. I announced that if he stopped kvetching and behaved himself at my parents', I'd give him a magnificent blow job on the drive home. Nothing like a positive incentive program to make everyone happy. As soon as we hit the freeway, I start stroking the already-large bulge in his pants. Then I unzip him, and his erection pops out. I suck him into my mouth and my head bobs up and down in his lap. Meanwhile he pulls off my top and unhooks my bra so that my breasts swing free. I love the way he gently fondles them as I continue to give him loving lip service. Our autoeroticism lasts about twenty miles, until we approach our exit, then he comes. I zip him up, which is why I'm writing. I worry that the zipper might pinch his tender flesh. He could zip himself up, but he really loves this little finishing touch, and I enjoy doing it for him. Any suggestions?

—C.H., Bowling Green, Ohio

Velcro? Simply reposition his penis down the leg of his trouser. Or, better yet, keep the fellatio up until you pull into your garage. Then you can complete the act with intercourse.

105. Bitch! Bitch! Bitch!

How dare you suggest that someone engage in fellatio while driving on a freeway! The twenty-mile blow job you described is unsafe sex. That attentive wife and her husband could kill someone.

—D.S., Los Angeles, California

Lighten up. The freeway fellatio the woman writer described seemed pretty safe—unless she was driving. People do all sorts of things in cars: A recent George Will column said that the California Office of Traffic Safety reports that "commuters are not just telephoning (there are 6.4 million cellular phones, up from half a million in 1986), they—the drivers—are brushing (and flossing) their teeth, diapering and nursing babies, mending clothes, eating baked potatoes and bowls of cereal." Some of them may even be reading George Will, though it's hard to imagine that they would be the ones getting fellated. The question is, how much attention does a blow job require? The brain processes about 126 bits of information per second. It takes about 40 bits of information per second to understand a simple conversation in English. (A neat experiment found that if you try to follow three conversations, you can—but you won't remember what the people were wearing, what they looked like, whatever.) Now, we don't know how many bits of information a blow job requires—that depends on the skill of the fellatrice—but we doubt if it's equivalent to trying to follow three conversations—unless maybe you are talking to your other girlfriend on the cellular phone. Do you black out after a blow job at home? Do you have to watch the action to believe it's happening to you? Then why do you think you would on the highway? There are hundreds of Japanese prints that show lovers doing very complicated acts—balancing things on their feet, shooting a bow and arrow—that suggest sex with the least amount of attention can be exciting.

106. Multiple Personality Masturbation

Okay. I know masturbation is not harmful, but is it possible to get too involved in solo sex? I sometimes act out fantasies—by myself. I let my facial expressions be those of my imaginary partner. Is this weird?

—F.D., San Francisco, California

We've read about guys who masturbate between mirrors so that when they come, a thousand images of themselves climax at the same time. Wow. Cosmic. Sex therapist Marty Klein, author of Ask Me Anything, *suggests that "moaning and other expressions of passion are normal during sex; since masturbation is sex, those expressions are appropriate during self-pleasure." Klein then quotes a poem by Ron Koertge:*

This is for every man who licks his shoulder during solitary sex

*rubs his beard against the stripy deltoid muscle or bites
  himself hard.*
*This is for the woman who at the body's buffet touches her
  breasts*
one at a time
*then reaches for the place she has made clean as mother's
  kitchen.*
*And please don't jump up afterward and rush for the
  washcloth*
like all the relatives were on the porch knocking
*their hands hot from casseroles and a cake with God's
  name on it.*
Rather lie there, catch your breath, turn to yourself
*and kiss all the nimble fingers, especially the one that has
  been you-know-where, kiss the palms with their mortal
  etchings and finally kiss the back of each hand*
*as if the Pope had just said that you are particularly
  blessed.*

Are we reassured yet?

107. How Civilized

Sometimes talking dirty doesn't work, and you can accomplish greater arousal through politeness. At least,
that's what Pierre Louys, author of *Manuel de civilité pour
les petites filles à l'usage des maisons d'education* may
have had in mind when he wrote the following in 1926:
"Never ask a man of the world: 'Fancy a blow job?' Only
little street girls express themselves like that. Instead,

whisper softly in his ear: 'Would you care to use my mouth?' "

108. The Eyes Have It

Sex therapists now suggest to clients that they make love while gazing into each other's eyes. We found a better description of the technique in a *Screw* magazine interview with porn star Marc Stevens. In response to a question about costar Tina Russell, he said, "She was the best I ever had. Tina put an incredible amount of love into her fucking. And God, what a cocksucker she was! She'd fuck my eyes with her eyes while she was sucking on me."

109. Foreplay Is Demeaning to Men

Some writers approach sex with a tongue-in-cheek attitude, which probably hinders oral sex, but what the hey. In 1977, Don R. King had fun with the topic of foreplay in *Sex Self Taught*. His approach:

One play: By prearrangement with your costar, deliberately act out a very fast, sudden fuck, cold turkey, in which you take the full initiative. With no preliminaries except to say 'hello' and with a dab of lubricant in case you are dry, start the action. . . . You will probably find that in a matter of seconds you are just as aroused as you have ever been, and there will be your proof that foreplay need is all in your head.

Two play: Stimulate yourself manually until you are aroused as you want to be, and then call your partner over for foreplay, which you will find you now don't need. Simple tests like this can be quite revealing.

Three play: With no preliminaries, not even a kiss, sit on your partner's chest, up high and present yourself for oral stimulation. You will probably turn on before you even get settled down, again proving that you are just a normal sexy female.

110. The Sex Trick We Wouldn't Publish

Some of the most inventive sex techniques come from the world of S&M. In 1993, Trevor Jacques published a thoughtful book called *On the Safe Edge*, in which he proposed the following:

What do you do if you are in a hotel and have no toys from home with you? In most hotel rooms there are hangers with clips for trousers. These clips can be adjusted to the distance between the nipples and used to great effect. Even better, they come with a pre-made hook for attaching weights (like your shoes or boots) or to pull upwards with your teeth.

The powers that be at *Playboy* thought this advice too strong to mention. Their feeling was that the sort of man who reads *Playboy* is not likely to try to duplicate the initiation scene from the movie *A Man Called Horse* [Richard Harris hanging from rawhide thongs sewn through his chest] in a hotel room. I argued that it defined a perfect sex trick: Whether or not you tried it, it changed forever the way you looked at hangers in hotel rooms.

111. The Full Frontal Frisk

Going from one extreme to the other, there are some authors who have explored gentleness as a sexual technique. Dr. Patricia Love and Jo Robinson, authors of *Hot Monogamy*, describe the joy of a light touch:

Hovering, which involves the lightest of touch, is done by holding your hands just above the surface of your mate's skin, brushing the fine hair. Many people find this a tantalizing experience. It can send chills up your spine and make you squirm with sensation. For the toucher it is a rare opportunity to focus completely on your mate. It can be a very sensual and loving experience.

112. Sea-Sharp Sex

Alex Comfort reinvented the sex manual, combining wonderful prose with erotic art. Others followed. In 1989,

Dr. Andrew Stanway came up with *The Art of Sensual Loving*, in which he described aquatic erotics:

Making love in deeper water can be highly arousing, though. Either the woman can lie back and cross her legs behind her lover's back as he enters her from in front, or she can stand waist high in the water and bend over to lie on it as he enters her from behind. A favorite position is to have the woman lie flat on her back floating so that her hips are at the level of his genitals. He now enters her and holding on to her hips, guides her body onto his penis. If you are far enough away from people this is a game that can be played even if you are not totally alone in the sea. Be sure not to lose your bikini bottom in the process. As holidays are such an ideal time for couples to behave romantically and to experiment with new locations, seaside sex can offer much pleasure.

113. Only If They're Hot

In 1986, *Playboy* interviewed Dr. Ruth Westheimer and discovered her secret to incredible sex:

A young man called and said, "Dr. Ruth, my girlfriend likes to toss fried onion rings on my erect penis." That permitted me to say, in a wonderful way, that I believe anything two consenting adults do in privacy is fine.

114. The Secret Turn-on

First we had *The Total Woman*. Then Dan Abeltow came up with *Total Sex*. His is one of the few sex manuals to address scent. Forget Calvin Klein's Obsession. Try this:

> This is an underhanded way for a woman to tell a man she wants him. It will blow all his gaskets at once. In a private moment (to obtain it, excuse yourself for a moment) insert your finger in your vagina. Hug him when you return, making sure to press his penis against your hips or side. As you do this put your arm around his neck and innocently pass your scented finger along his top lip, just under his nose. Chances are, either his eyes will pop out of his head or he'll choke on his heart which will have jumped into his throat. Whisper in a sultry voice that you can't wait until you get home. In less than 30 seconds the bulge in his pants will show that he can't wait either.

115. Dial "M" for Master

Working our way through the alphabet, after *The Sensuous Woman* by J and on the way to *The Story of O*, we find *The Sensuous Man* by "M." He entered the sex-tricks sweepstakes with a pair of winners:

The Strawberry Suckle

Sprinkle the breasts with soft kisses and then follow up with nibbling of the aureole (dark circle around the nipple). Now, slip your tongue over the same area, circling the nipple faster, faster, faster (as if you were running around and around in a revolving door). Next, draw the nipple into your mouth, knead it gently and then begin sucking, pulling as much of the breast into your mouth as you can, pressing it firmly between the tongue and roof of your mouth. Suck as a baby does while being fed. Repeat all steps many times, alternating from breast to breast.

The Runaway Pinch

This one is a quickie in the truest sense. Take the tips of your thumb and index finger and bring them together as if they were a pair of foam-rubber tweezers: open, shut, open, shut. Then using this gentle tweezing action, begin very lightly and quickly pinching her behind, thighs, stomach, nipples, arms, legs—everywhere you can reach. Be sure to move your fingers like streaked lightning, or you won't produce the desired effect.

The Runaway Pinch can also be done with your mouth. Just be sure to stretch your lips until they cover the sharp edges of your teeth to avoid inadvertently nicking or cutting her soft skin.

116. The Violin Bow Effect

John Eichenlaub followed *The Art of Marriage* with a second bestseller, *New Approaches to Sex in Marriage*. This time the art was music:

> You stimulate your wife quite keenly when you draw the shaft of your penis across the upper edge of her female organ. This type of friction at this particular site brings her sexual sensations unmatched by other action. You can use it in most sexual positions, but especially in the pillow trick [pillow placed under small of back to elevate clitoris], usual, and asymmetrical face to face postures or the twisted trunk rear entry position. . . . Like the violin bow rubbing a string, which gives just as loud a note when moved slowly, shaft to inner lip friction stimulates just as keenly whether movement is slow or fast. However, the first inch or so of either an inward or outward stroke gives very little of this type friction, since the inner lips initially move along with the shaft instead of being rubbed by it. After these highly sensitive folds have been turned all the way in or out, further movement in the same direction stimulates a stretched out extensive surface both with friction and vibration by: 1. Sliding your body headward to increase pressure on the sensitive parts. 2. Using long strokes both inward and outward. 3. Slow motion, especially in the mid phase of each stroke. Some husbands stimulate their wives most effectively with a sort of "stutter movement" giving a quick motion at the beginning of each inward or outward stroke (to turn the wife's inner lips in the right direction) followed by a long, slow movement the rest of the way.

Others find slow movement on a regular rhythm easier, especially if the wife is making reciprocal movements of her own.

117. The Cat and the Fiddle

Not to be outdone, Dr. Irene Kasorla also reached for a musical metaphor in *Nice Girls Do*:

At any point when the tide recedes and the man has a soft-on, he can maintain his partner's level of excitement in the orgasmic continuum by keeping her going. He can do this by using his soft-on or the rest of his body: his hands and mouth can stimulate her clitoris and nipples; his lips and tongue can enjoy the feeling of kissing her and being kissed.

It's important for him to contact as many of her erogenous zones as possible. For example, when one of his fingers is inside his lover's vagina, his thumb is on her clitoris, his other hand is fondling her breasts, and he's kissing her mouth—four erogenous zones are being stimulated simultaneously. The more areas he can touch on, the more orgasms she will experience.

One way to do this is by getting into what I call the "Bass Fiddle" position.

The man lies on his side, facing and holding his partner, who is on her back lying right next to him. Her hips are crossing over his hips, positioned so that she can feel his soft penis on the upper back side of her thighs, near her vagina. The upper part of his left arm is underneath her shoulders and the lower part of this arm comes around, leaving his left hand free to cover her breast. His right hand can then massage (and or penetrate) her vagina, anus and clitoris. He plays her body as a musician would play a bass fiddle.

118. The Naked Neilsen Rating

Regarding your plea for sex tips, tricks (and traps?) I submit the following somewhat romantic way to spend an evening with your partner. If the two (or more) of you happen to be interested in erotic films, I've found that a great way to make the experience all the more erotic is to view the film naked, under a duvet (comforter in American English) whilst slowly caressing and holding your partner's genitalia (or other erotic bits). The basic idea is that by keeping a "finger on the pulse" of your lover's eroticism, you can get an idea of what in the film really turns him or her on. Of course, most people can't continue to do this without getting carried away and making love or having some other "fun," but that is why the nice people who make VCRs include a pause button. I have done this with several of my lovers in the past, and the experience really is amazing. Sitting there holding each other, stroking, watching, yet keeping warm and somewhat secretive under the duvet—it adds something mysterious to it, an element of fantasy.

—S.M., the Internet

119. The Flashback

I have something that really isn't a position or a trick. It all started when a friend suggested making love to a black light. Well, that was quite erotic and sensual. But one night all we had was the flash to my camera. Just for the heck of it, we just started flashing the light. It would leave us with interesting images of each other. They would only last a sec, but we found it to be very sensual. We then began playing with different filters. The blue seemed to do the best job. Caution: It isn't very good for your eyes. So don't do it long or often.

—M.J., the Internet

120. The Treehouse

My girlfriend and I were at a party at a friend's house the summer before our junior year of college. My girlfriend and I were enjoying ourselves, basking in the late-evening glow after a day of food and friends at a beer and barbecue party with about fifty other people. As the evening turned to night and the stars began to fill the sky, the happy mood shared by me and my girlfriend turned romantic and lustful. We considered leaving the party so we could go spend time alone, but almost simultaneously we remembered there was a tree fort in the front yard of the house. One of us, I don't remember which, suggested checking out the treehouse to see what it was like. We went out into the yard and climbed up the makeshift ladder to the deck of the fort.

The tree fort was basically just a floor and a bench nailed to the limbs of a large maple tree for support. While up in the fort, we could feel the cool breeze of the night air and hear the music and buzz of the party below us. We also quickly realized no one knew we were in the fort. The fort had been a center of activity for most of the afternoon, but now it was left to us. High up in the fort, we felt secluded from the rest of the party, and we kissed. The kissing grew more passionate and intense, and the desire and urgency flooded our bodies. We had a quick discussion.

"Here?" I asked.

"Can anyone see us?" she asked.

"I don't know. I think so."

"Ah, fuck it, who cares," she said, as she undid my belt.

I slid her panties down underneath her skirt and we made love quickly, fighting the urge to laugh out loud, giggling "I love you" to each other.

—T.K., the Internet

121. The Inner Orgasm

My Thai wife showed me a special meditation technique a few years ago when we were driving to a deserted beach on the border to Burma. It was in the afternoon and my wife asked me to sit down and watch. After meditating for some forty-five minutes sitting cross-legged in a lotus position on the beach, she took off her clothes and went into the warm water. Getting on her knees in a doggie position, she continued to meditate but this time by slowly starting to move her hips in slow motion. She told me later that she was completely relaxed, with the focus on the invisible forces making love with her. She did not touch herself, and only the water and the wind touched her body. After some fifteen minutes she reached a powerful orgasm and I could finally join her for the next hour when the sun set over the Indian Ocean.

—I.M., the Internet

122. The Love Boat

My wife and I made love in the hot tub of a cruise ship. While that may not be so unusual, there were about six young women (between 20 and 23 years old, I would guess) in the hot tub right next to ours, no more than twelve feet away, who tried not to let us know that they were watching. Knowing they were made it very exciting.

—J.T., the Internet

123. The Lower Case

ABCs! Using the information I learned as a young boy, I've finally put it to a very good use as an adult. I simply use my tongue to spell out the ABCs during a fellatio session and I guarantee this will bring her to orgasm. Don't forget there are also lowercase abc's!

Good luck, love the magazine. Demonstrations given on a first-come, first-served basis. Aloha.

—P.I., the Internet

This used to be a joke in Sam Kinneson's stand-up routine. Contributors also suggested Hebrew letters and Chinese written characters. See if he or she can decipher the sentence.

124. The Piano Bench

My lover lives in a single-room apartment, with a futon on the floor. I found that the lower level of the futon facilitated some sex acts—our tussles were closer to wrestling matches, and to push your lover over the edge was a great thrill. But as a side benefit, the absence of a bed made us improvise sex acts on other pieces of furniture. I have laid her over the piano bench, kneeling between her legs—the height of the padded seat is perfect. Her feet touch the floor, and I have unimpeded access to her clitoris. When she is aroused, I rise to a kneeling position and enter. Then again, I can lie on the bench, and she stand above me. With feet still touching the floor, she can pivot, dance, or gallop. My question: Does anybody sell benches just for lovemaking?

—R.P., Del Mar, California

You don't think all the people who buy Soloflex equipment are in it for their pecs, do you? Weight benches have the added plus of an inclined platform. You have stumbled onto a major flaw to modern living. The people who design beds design them for sleeping. You could raise your bed to the height of, say, a pool table—which at least would put your partner on a plane with your erection when standing. We recall reading one manual that suggested taking sexual measurements—your height and hers, standing and kneeling—to build special furniture, or design alcoves with sex in mind. Another expert suggested leaving a short stool in the bedroom—yes, a milking stool—so that one person could have an island off the edge of the bed.

125. The Piano

I read your letter about using piano benches as sexual furniture. I once had a lover who kept an old upright piano in her living room. With the cover closed, it was the perfect height for her to sit legs spread, arms supported along the top. We tried it once or twice with her sitting directly on the keys—but it was both uncomfortable and discordant. The position works for both oral sex (remember the long shot in *Pretty Woman*) and stride piano (standing).

—F.T., New York, New York

126. The Recline and Fall

The best sex trick that I ever tried was to lay my girlfriend on her back on a rocking recliner, while I knelt in front of the recliner facing her. As we made love, I would rock the recliner, which made the power of my thrusts stronger and also helped to produce a kind of rhythm that always makes her orgasm.

—C.H., the Internet

127. Location, Location, Location

In response to your question: Does place matter? Let's see, I've made love in parks late at night, in a room full of people (a hostel), on the walkway around a short lighthouse, in a moving car with me driving, in every room of a house, in a sailboat, on a new mattress before it was unpacked, in a bathroom at work, in a church parking lot (on a Sunday), at a college library. You know, as often as I have tried variations on certain themes or whatever, I find the only thing that has to be in place is me and my love, and both of us wanting to exhaust each other. The place is special for memory, I suppose, but who cares about place when the orgasms are given to each other by each other?

—D.K., the Internet

128. Keeping Place

To my wife, place apparently doesn't matter. Or maybe it does matter. She has been known to give head in the ladies' room of a public park (late in the season, after all of the kiddies are in school). The best places we have had a quickie (or not so quickie) have been on balconies/patios. The first time was on the patio of a special couples' love nest hotel, the second was on the balcony of our current flat. So I guess outdoors is a good place.

—M.B., the Internet

129. Clit Lit Review

A few years ago I sat down to write a review of feminist erotica. Here's what I discovered about women's sexual imagination: The stories share a sense of adventure. Characters make love in oceans, lakes, rivers, and swimming pools, in the backs of pickup trucks, on trains, buses, bent over tires in gas stations, handcuffed to beds, on the tops of tables and desks, on beaches, in cliff side tents, in back country stores, on living room couches and oh, yes, occasionally in bed. And the men in the stories are bold. Here is one talking:

I was at a rock concert one time, thousands of people packed in close together all standing up to see better and moving, kind of dancing in place because there wasn't room to do anything else. I was with this girl ∴.. she had on a really short skirt, like yours, and one time when she dropped her purse and bent over to pick it up I saw she wasn't wearing any underpants. So . . . I got her to stand in front of me and I unzipped and slipped it in, and slowly, easily pumped away. Nobody knew what we were doing. Even when we both came nobody noticed, because everybody was yelling and hopping around.

130. The Fist

Even when a writer describes sex with a supernatural lover, there are things to learn. The narrator of Kate Robinson's "Silver, Gold, Red, Black" in *Herotica 2* gave this description of fisting:

> The shape's hands are on my pubis now. Its fingers trail between my inner lips, invade my vagina. One hand balls up and thrusts into me, the other grips my ass. Its fist snakes rudely upwards inside me, the knuckles kneading my walls, which roll and squeeze against them. A stand-up bass thrum descends from my uterus to my vagina.

131. How the Cliterati Masturbate

As I read through feminist erotica—the stories collected by Susie Bright, Michelle Slung, and Lonnie Barbach—I was struck by the power of hands, how if one put one's imagination into an act as simple as masturbation, it could be as compelling as intercourse. Here's how one member of the cliterati combined cool lotion and memory to fill the moment with heat:

> The lotion is cool as it touches your fingers and you pause for a moment, anticipating the sensation when you reach between your legs. It is even colder there. It

is wonderful. You spread it eagerly between the folds of skin and over the one most sensitive spot. . . . Close your eyes and imagine him now, being with him in a way you have never been. Think what it would be like if he were swirling his tongue where his hand has been and you clutching the sides of his head with your thighs, his shaggy brown hair wet against your skin. He is licking slowly from bottom to top in long ice cream cone swipes. Your own tongue goes out to lick the air as you envision his, searching through every crevice. Your hand is in his mouth, and then his lips, sucking around that unnamed spot, nibbling, seeking devouring around and around so warm and wet until you burst and writhe and whisper, almost too loud, Fuck me! Fuck me, now!

132. The Daredevil

I saw a posting you had about asking where people have made love or something to that effect. Well, I am sure these are all normal places, so don't be surprised to find something out of the ordinary. Pool table, couch below parents' bedroom, bed over parents' bedroom, various cars, shower, cramped closet, backseat of car that parents were driving (although this was not full lovemaking . . . it did get to oral sex and fondling). So that is a brief list. So far.

—S.C., the Internet

133. The Drill Team

The following secret was given to me by a sixty-four-year-old sergeant major in the U.S. Army Reserves: While performing oral sex on your partner, use your pinky finger to stimulate (not necessarily penetrate) your partner's anus. It works like a charm every time. I'm sorry, but I don't have a name for it . . . call it what you like . . . I guess I could call it "it works."

—J.A., the Internet

134. The French Twist

"*La friandise*," I think that's how you spell it. This movement was perhaps the thing of greatest value that I learned in the eleventh grade on my foreign exchange stint in France. Jean-Paul, my nineteen-year-old lover, was quite into *la friandise* . . . To "*faire la friandise*," the man is inserting his fingers into the woman, but with a twisting motion, twisting his fingers over and over again.

—W.L., the Internet

135. Dial "O" for Orgasm

I'm not sure if this is well known or not, but one thing that drives my lover wild is when I touch her cervix in a circular motion. I used to have a difficult time bringing her to orgasm but now I can make her come in five minutes.

—M.K., the Internet

136. The Birthday Gift

My husband's fortieth birthday is coming up, and I want to do something special for him. He has wanted to try anal intercourse for a long time, but I've always nixed it. I tried it once, long before I met him, and it hurt; hence my reluctance. But, with his birthday around the corner, I checked a sex manual that stressed the need for good lubrication during anal intercourse and realized that my previous experience had been completely unlubricated. This time, I'll have the K-Y handy. Is there anything else I should know about the anal alternative to make it fun for both of us?

—L.M., St. Paul, Minnesota

Using lubrication definitely puts you on the right track. Lack of it was probably the major reason you had difficulty the first time. But how you use your lubricant is also important. Apply it generously around the rectum and internally as far as your finger can comfortably reach. Also apply some to your husband's penis—both head and shaft. Some people believe that the penis can be adequately lubricated with saliva during oral foreplay, but in our experience, saliva won't get the job done. Once both of you are ready, try one of two positions: you on your hands and knees at the edge of the bed with your husband standing behind you, or you on your stomach with a pillow under your hips and him kneeling behind you. You should control the action from there. Push out with your rectal muscles as you take his erection in hand and guide it in slowly. As you guide him in, breathe deeply to keep yourself relaxed. There's no need to take in his entire erection on one motion. Accept the head of his penis, pause, then work his shaft in slowly, a half inch or so at a time. You may feel comfortable taking it all the way in. Or, beyond a certain point you may begin to experience discomfort no matter how well lubricated you both are. Let him know when you've reached your comfort limit. Then let go of his penis and invite him to move. At first, he should move very slowly, but as you get used to the motion, let him know when he can move more freely. As either of you approaches climax, let the other know. That's when he should withdraw partway, because orgasm hip thrusts may push him in deeper than your comfort limit. Finally, be sure that both of you wash thoroughly before resuming vaginal contact.

137. The Receiving Line

Try entering your lover's nest inch by inch. At each level stop and ask if that is enough. Wait for her answer. She goes crazy. And you say it is your honor to move only when asked.

—J.U., the Internet

138. The Jujube

I think the simplest sex trick that works the best is to put a piece of candy—a Jujube, Life Saver, or Jujyfruit—on your partner's clitoris, close your eyes, and enjoy. I think you will find that when the Jujyfruit is finished this is a good example of a "Win/Win Situation." For some reason, the trick works well during fellatio, too—I guess anything that creates saliva increases the old slipping and sliding feeling.

—C.R., the Internet

139. Ravenous Ravioli

I have recently heard of an unusual sexual practice taking place in the hills above Rome on Friday evenings. Single females place their best homemade ravioli in auspicious places, hoping to attract members of the opposite sex. Once drawn to the ravioli, the males begin to eat, at which time groups of hungry females surround and tie down the single males. One woman, usually the one responsible for the preparation of the ravioli, will have the first opportunity to orally stimulate him in an ancient Roman manner which involves the usage of hot ravioli held between the woman's tongue and the foreskin of the male.

—P.A., the Internet

140. Tongue-Tied

I used to be a professional musician, playing both brass instruments and keys. From my efforts I developed a few abilities that paid off well when it came to sex. The first I called the triple-tonguing. Wind instrumentalists use a method of separating notes called tonguing, with variations called double- and triple-tonguing. (To double-tongue, make your tongue move as if you are saying Tah-kah, to triple-tongue say Tah-kah-dah.) The use is fairly simple; gently suck your date's clit into your mouth and then start the above method. It works really well if you can circular breathe as well. (Note, it also works great on nipples.)

The second I called trilling. A keyboardist does a two-note trill by rapidly moving two fingers on two different notes. I found that by gently inserting two fingers into my partner's vagina and then moving my fingers in a trilling fashion along the top side of her vaginal wall (top being the side nearest her pubic mound), I'd have my lover coming in huge spasms.

—E.M., the Internet

141. Red Light, Green Light

When my lover and I are making love and she gets to her orgasmic peak I take my cock out of her suddenly. She lies there a moment wondering what has just happened. I act as if I don't notice the fact that she didn't want the passion to end. Then just as she starts to almost be offended, I reinsert my cock and I "go at it" like I never have before. At that point the sex is the best it has ever been.

—P.T., the Internet

142. The Overlay

My favorite trick is a position in which I lie on my side facing my partner and she lies on her back with her knees over my hips. This allows me to be inside her, yet leaves my hands free to massage her at the same time. We usually start with my stroking her clitoris, and then move to this position, where we can have intercourse at the same time I directly stimulate her clitoris. This appears to induce a very intense orgasm (and it's fun for me too!).

—B.D., the Internet

143. The Squeeze Play

One thing that works for my girlfriend and me as an alternate approach (we only use it once every few weeks) is to have her lie on her back with her legs together, and then I enter her from a straddling position. Just rearranging our legs from the missionary position like this has led to some incredible orgasms for both of us—I blacked out the first time (couldn't see, not passed out).

Hope it helps someone else, too.

—F.C., the Internet

144. When It Rains

Lubrication during sex has never been difficult for me. In fact, I get so wet, I lose all sensation and can hardly feel my boyfriend inside of me. He won't say so, but I know sensation becomes a problem for him, too. Short of stopping to towel myself off, what can I do?

—P.L., Miami Beach, Florida

One easy solution is to press your partner's penis gently but firmly between your thumb and forefinger as he thrusts. The benefits are twofold: It creates more friction for him and positions your hand so that you are free to masturbate. But there's nothing wrong with interrupting the action long enough for you and your partner to keep your moisture in check. Don't limit yourself to terrycloth. Think feathers, fur, velvet, and silk. There's plenty of erotic potential in the interlude, and the beauty of it is that you get to start all over again.

145. The Kitchen Timer

Several of the tricks in this book depend on spontaneity and urgency. The quickie has its place, but what of the opposite? Most sex manuals by and for women advocate languid lovemaking. (Even instructions for autoeroticism suggest taking a long warm bath, with candles, romantic music, and wine. They bring romance to solo sex! Add a partner to that scenario and you have the beginning of a great long evening.) Male authors are catching on. Donald Norfolk, author of *Sex Drive*, describes one method:

> This is a test of mind over matter which requires the aid of a kitchen timer. Wind the clock and set the alarm to ring after thirty minutes. During this time you and your partner must lie naked together, in a position of full penetration, without reaching a climax. For that half hour you can kiss, pet and fondle, but you must otherwise lie still without moving your pelvis or attempting to reach an orgasm. This practice is very similar to carezza . . . or coitus reservatus, with one delightful difference: when the alarm rings you don't separate, but proceed to a climax which is often all the more intense because of the prolonged period of arousal and enforced self-control.

The ticking might add suspense. There are other ways to keep time. Light a candle. Undress. Explore each other for as long as the candle burns. When it sputters, go for your climax in the dark.

146. Creative Lighting

My wife likes to make love in just about total darkness. I like more light—not bright overhead light, but the reading lamp or a candle. Can you suggest a compromise?

—E.L., Oceanside, New York

Stop looking at sexual lighting as an either-or proposition. Instead, play with the lighting as you play with each other. Open the curtains and let some moonlight in. Give your wife a blindfold and turn all the lights on. (Hey, you can even catch a game on TV and she won't know.) Camp out and see what sex is like under starlight. Or during lovemaking light a match, and after a few seconds, have your wife blow it out.

147. Here, Darling, You Park It

A good way to find out when your partner is fully aroused? Invite her to initiate penetration. Put your erection into her hand and let her guide you into her—when and only when she is ready. It might take days. She may take you for long walks around the bedroom.

148. Read This One Aloud

Louis Meldman wrote a fine exploration of *Mystical Sex* in which he argued that Westerners deprive themselves of a larger, oceanic form of sex by focusing on the active. If you simply let things happen, you can experience a different kind of sex:

In mystical sex, lovers need to make no effort, furious, furtive, conscious, or otherwise, to thrust, hump, pump, jump, bump and grind, rub, writhe, wriggle, wiggle, shimmy or shake, sock, knock, rock and roll. Swinging, swaying, pressing, pushing, plunging, pulling, wham, bam, slam, bang, tango, fandango, mamba, hula, boogaloo, cha-cha-cha! You don't have to think about those or any other motions if you let your natural, instinctive, inner knowledge take you along, a long way past such regular basic fucking. Thank you, ma'am! Lifting, sinking, in-out, way out, way in, up-down, around-and-around, side to side, to sidesaddle, high in the saddle, bareback, way back, backbone slip. "If I hold you any closer, we'll be in back of each other," quipped Groucho Marx. Back and forth, linear, circular, rotating, revolving, vibrating, figure eight, parabolic, peristaltic, gyroscopic, oceanic, or as songwriter Warren Zevon put it, "like a Waring blender"—it's still regular pedestrian sex as long as one is carrying out, executing or consciously performing such actions. It is the effort itself, the willing, the very striving to do it in such and such a way, just so, on purpose, that will prevent one from reaching the altered emotional play of mystical experience.

149. Tying the Knot

I'm a twenty-six-year-old heterosexual female who has never had an orgasm with a male. However, I can have an orgasm through what is probably the most unusual way a woman can masturbate. I ball up a piece of sheet or cloth until it is a hard knot the size of a baseball. While on my stomach, I put the hard knot under my vagina and rub on it. I believe because of my unusual way of masturbating, I cannot have an orgasm during intercourse in any position. Any suggestions?

—D.S., Kansas City, Kansas

Why not tie the bedclothes into a knot, assume the position, and have your partner enter you from the rear. Or, while he is still dressed, pull his erection out to the side, mount, and twist his underwear with your fist.

150. Nearly Nude

Sex in the nude is fun, but lately my wife and I have discovered the special turn-on of doing it clothed—not just in pajamas or lingerie but fully dressed in business attire. We've been wearing loose clothes for easy access: boxer shorts and pleated slacks for me, and for her, billowy blouses, front-closing bras, and flared skirts with stockings instead of panty hose. Any suggestions?

—B.R., Creve Coeur, Missouri

Why limit yourself to business attire? Try doing it in baggy warm-up suits, stretchy beachwear, old gardening duds, or the costumes you wore to your last masquerade party. We can imagine a wonderful evening spent digging into each other's closets for clothes to model and test for easy access, especially anything you no longer wear. Try cutting out pockets and crotches. That way you can reach a hand through to stimulate your partner or yourself in a crowded elevator.

151. The Sounds of Sex

Help! I think I'm perverted. I love to go to a cheap motel and listen to people having sex in other rooms. I love to hear those squeaky beds creaking. What a turn-on. Am I weird? Also, I love dirty movies but mostly I listen rather than look. Sometimes I can't help but look, but mostly it's the moaning and groaning that turns me on. When my boyfriend eats my pussy, it's the sound that makes me come. That slurping, that sucking, that gulping. I'm getting turned on just thinking about it. I've mentioned the motel trip to a few friends and they all think I'm sick. But I say it's harmless, safe sex.

—A.D., San Francisco, California

Why not? Sex is part friction, part fantasy. There are only so many nerve endings and so many ways to touch them. By opening up your mind to psychological stimulation—the sounds of sex—you can pump up the volume. We know of one artist who created an installation of boom boxes, Dictaphone, hand-held tape recorders, CB radios, and full-scale stereos—each blasting out a separate sexual encounter taped from movies, telephone sex, and real life. It was an aural tapestry that still echoes. Or check out the erotic CD called Cyborgasm *by Lisa Palac and friends, or* Sounds of Sex *by Ava Cadell. They are a series of sexual vignettes that rival the best of NPR—you can make a drive tape for rush hour.*

152. Locker-room Sex

My girlfriend and I were on the beach near Montauk Point, Long Island. It was rather secluded. After swimming in the ocean, we went back to our blanket to towel off. While doing so, I rolled my towel into a "rattail" and, though I intended to give her just a love tap, I managed to produce an audible, crisp, whiplike snap. The towel barely kissed her muscular ass, but that was enough. Her entire body went taut, she turned to face me, her eyes squeezed shut, her lips puckered small and tight; she felt the pain. I just stood there. I didn't know what to do. Then her lips curved slightly upward at the corners and she whispered in a challenging tone, "Didn't hurt." Her defiant statement earned her one on the other cheek. It had the same effect. She drew a long deep breath through her nose and said, "Take me home." We packed up, drove home in silence, and took showers. When I stepped out of the shower, I was confronted by my smirking girlfriend in her birthday suit. She rolled the towel she had in her hands and tried to whip me with it, but it only wrapped around my knee. She giggled and tossed the towel at me and said, "Your turn." She then turned around and placed her hands on the door frame, legs spread apart. I repeated the action that had taken place on the beach earlier, leaving matching marks below the ones already there (being a college lacrosse player, I was well practiced in such locker-room antics). She took the towel from my hands, put it around my neck, and dragged me into the bedroom. She pushed me onto the bed and began sucking my cock like a champ. At times she had my entire cock in her mouth—she'd never been able to do that before. While she was doing this, I spanked her. The harder I spanked, the more enthusiastically she sucked me. By the time I came I was spanking her so hard my hand was hurting. She swallowed every drop of come she could suck out of me. This is a girl who repeatedly told me she would never swallow, that it was too gross to even think about. So what gives? Why did pain turn her on? Would you please touch on the basics of sadomasochistic behavior?

—S.E., Chester, Pennsylvania

Okay, America, are we hot yet? We don't think we need to touch on the basics regarding sadomasochistic behavior. Your letter pretty much covered them all. A partner, thrilled at being a sexual outlaw, led you into new territory. She set the pace and directed the action, and you both enjoyed the result.

153. Telephone Sex

I recently met a rather kinky and intriguing twenty-eight-year-old professional guy who lives in the condo next to mine. I am twenty-six and quite sexual. I find my neighbor interesting and challenging. We haven't had intercourse yet because I don't want to rush things, but we have had intense oral and phone sex on several occasions. In one particular instance his best friend called while we were fooling around on the sofa. My neighbor handed me the phone. His friend proceeded to ask me to take off my clothes, touch myself in various spots, and describe the outrageous oral sex that my neighbor was suddenly performing on me. I agreed to all of this and climaxed while on the phone, which obviously turned the friend on immensely. Now the two of them want to have a threesome, saying that they have done this twice in the past with significant others. Should I consider this an experiment?

—J.D., Newark, New Jersey

We've seen this scenario in quite a few X-rated flicks (The Seduction of Mary, Cat and Mouse, Firestorm). Maybe Ma Bell has a new campaign: Reach out and ask someone to touch herself. Before you try the real thing, perhaps you ought to have an obscene conference call to work out the details. For now, this telephonic turn-on seems harmless and horny. On the other hand, none of their significant others are still around.

154. Erotic Swings

Where can I find erotic swings—devices that you hang from ceiling hooks for gravity-free sex?

—T.K., San Diego, California

The Xandria Collection sells something called the Love Hammock for about $120 (call 800-242-2823), while Good Vibrations offers a well-thought-out hanging chair called the Pleasure Swing for $235 (call 415-974-8990 or 800-289-8423). The ad copy for the latter suggests the reason these things are so popular: "As any hammock fan can testify, there's nothing like being suspended in midair to create a relaxed, receptive state of mind and body." You can enter your partner and let the swing do the work. Or simply stand in one place and let your erection graze the lips of your lover's genitals. The swing also works for oral sex—the rush *of blood to the head can make for dizzying debauchery. We've also seen some intriguing variations on this theme: A dance troupe in San Francisco uses rock climbers' harnesses for aerial ballet. Imagine Wendy and Peter Pan doing it and you'll see the possibilities.*

155. Catalog Sex

Have you ever heard of a ball stretcher? A guy at work says it's like a cock ring, except that it's worn around the testicles.

—F.W., New York, New York

Uptown Toys and Treasures, the catalog for Romantasy (199 Moulton Street, San Francisco, CA 94123), lists a combination cock ring and ball stretcher (it looks like two leather bracelets connected) with this explanation: "While many people are familiar with the benefits of a cock ring (men may experience sustained erections once the ring is snugly applied), the effects of a ball stretcher are less well known. This combination in black leather snaps first against the base of the body with the cock and balls pushed forward. The testicles then are pulled downward while the stretcher is snapped around that skin area. The stretcher does not allow the balls to elevate, thus creating a delicious pressure or tension during sexual play." If you want to duplicate the sensation, have your lover tug on your testicles as she would the strap on a subway. Or you can use one half of a pair of handcuffs. Eat your heart out, Madonna.

156. Cough Drops

Recently, while recovering from a severe cold, I sucked on mentholated cough drops for my scratchy throat—twenty-four hours a day. When my girlfriend and I went to bed that evening, I went down on her as usual, but my breath was still affected by the menthol. To my surprise, she went wild, screaming so loudly I thought the neighbors would hear. She had the most intense orgasm I have ever witnessed. When she recovered fifteen minutes later, I blew lightly on her and she immediately had another orgasm. After further exploration, we concluded that the cough drops were the spice in this incredible experience. Can mentholated cough drops cause any medical problems?

—J.B., Brookhaven, Mississippi

You can use cough drops to enhance your sexual plea-sure, as long as you lick the plate clean. (Otherwise you might upset the pH balance of the vagina.) Bon appetit.

157. Whatever Happened to Drive-ins?

Down here in our little corner of Texas, things are heating up at the local adult theaters. It seems that quite a few couples, including us, are engaging in the time-honored tradition of show-and-don't-tell when the lights are low. These are mostly planned performances, which can range from the relatively tame showing of skin to raucous gymnastics over the seats. We were at one recently where the audience of ten or so gave the couple a standing ovation as they left. Do you know if this is a trend in other parts of the country? Is it legal?

—J.O., El Paso, Texas

Hello, does the name Pee Wee Herman mean anything to you?

158. Sandpaper?

My nipples are one of my major erogenous zones, second only to my clitoris. I can almost climax from stimulation of my nipples alone. The problem: My nipples are rather insensitive to light or normal touch. I like to attach clips to my nipples or twist them hard, burn them lightly with candle wax, or rough them up with sandpaper. I found that if I do this prior to sex with my husband, my nipples are so sensitive I can feel every touch and suck. The next day they're still so sensitive I can hardly keep my hands off myself, and frankly, I do not try. Am I doing permanent damage to myself?

—K.C., Portland, Maine

We've heard of safecrackers who sand the callouses off their fingertips—the better to feel the combination click in. And years ago we got a letter from a guy who masturbated with sandpaper. He asked if he had a problem. We said, "Yes, but not for long." Apparently he consulted a sex therapist who cured him of the habit by switching to lighter grades of sandpaper, velvet, then a real woman. He still gets a hard-on every time he passes Ace Hardware, but they're working on that. You are abusing your body, but so does every person who runs a marathon, mounts a StairMaster, or plays tennis. Are sexual injuries the same as athletic injuries? It's your call. All you've done is found a dramatic way to amplify the signals going to the brain.

159. Oral Exercises

I know a motorcycle mechanic who claims that he practices for cunnilingus by removing the corks from champagne bottles with his tongue. Kenneth Ray Stubbs and Chyrell D. Chasen had a better exercise in their book *The Clitoral Kiss*:

Repeat L words such as lust, lewd, lascivious. Suck a licorice string. Practice touching your nose with your tongue. Lick lots of lollipops. Dial your telephone with your tongue. Suck and tongue the jelly out of a donut. Tie cherry stems with your tongue. Remove your lover's clothes with just your mouth. Hang an orange on a string and practice martial arts with your tongue. Jab the orange. Lift it up with an upward sliding motion. Slap it from side to side. After a few weeks graduate to a grapefruit. And to prepare for the Olympics, practice with a jar filled with weights.

160. Body Heat

My wife and I like our sex hot—and cold. We turn off the air conditioning, which heats things up, then she slides ice cubes all over my hot body, and I do the same to her. Trouble is, the ice melts and makes a mess. Do you know a way to get iced without getting wet?

—F.T., Key West, Florida

We've had fun with the chemical and/or refreezable ice packs athletic trainers use on sports injuries. They're less messy than plain ice. They also stay cold longer and they can be molded around interesting parts of the body. Get one at a pharmacy or sporting goods store. If the food-sex scene in Nine ½ Weeks *turned you on, try a bag of frozen raspberries. Leave them in the bag, or feed them to each other. As for the messiness factor, we like to break out the oils, lotions, and ice cubes the night before we do laundry.*

161. Advanced Nipple Play

My girlfriend's breasts seem to be incredibly erogenous. She can have an orgasm just from foreplay, but it has to be fairly vigorous. Can you suggest some techniques?

—D.E., New Orleans, Louisiana

How weird do you want it? Aficionados will use anything that causes an unusual sensation—ice cubes, sheepskin, toothbrushes, hairbrushes, gardening gloves, or chopsticks drawn across the nipple. We recently read a hilarious cat- alog of accessories in On the Safe Edge *by Trevor Jacques: "You'd be surprised how many household objects can be used for tit play. The most common are clothespins." And all we ever use them for is laundry.*

162. Blue Confessions

My husband has become very curious about the men I slept with prior to our marriage. I have never been comfortable discussing them because he knows there were quite a few. But during a recent lovemaking session he kept asking me the same nagging questions. I told him a detailed story about a past lover and me. The result was the most exciting sex that we've ever had. Now once a week I recall a past experience and we do it all over again. Will these recollections backfire on me at a later date?

—N.A., Pittsburgh, Pennsylvania

We doubt it. We're not sure what's going on, but aural sex is a growth industry in America. Talking dirty fuels phone sex, computer sex, books-on-tape sex, confessional sex (if you're Catholic; sex therapy if you're secular), and now this. You don't have to describe your past lovers to turn your husband on. You'll probably get the same result by describing your own fantasies or even by pretending to be Siskel or Ebert recounting the plots of favorite porn flicks. Why is this so exciting? To paraphrase Sherlock Holmes, sex is not what happens, it's what you notice. By recounting a story you tell your lover what was memorable, what you liked to do, what you liked done to you. It turns your body into a library of lusty stories; every time your husband makes love to your breasts, he is seeing them as desired by others.

163. Creative Lusting 101

I'm always on the lookout for new ways to make love, but it seems that I've run out of ideas. Any suggestions?

—F.W., Alexandria, Virginia

Give a man a fish, you feed him for one day. Teach a man to fish, you feed him for a lifetime. Teach a man to fuck and he'll give up fishing forever. What you need is a short course in creative thinking. Start with the basic variations: If you usually close your eyes as you approach orgasm, next time look your partner in the eye. Like to have sex in a parked car? Try it in one that's moving. Like to have sex in the dark on a comfy bed? Try lovemaking on a high-backed chair under a spotlight. Another approach is to exaggerate one aspect of lovemaking: Pretend the area behind your lover's knee is the entire sexual universe. Spend a long afternoon there. Or take away one of the ingredients and see what's left. Wear a blindfold. Make love without using your hands. Tell your partner she cannot move. Finally, do the same old thing in new locations—after a Broadway play, in a hotel suite with room service. Sometimes the ideas that produce the best sex happen outside the sex act.

164. Surprise!

One evening last week I found a note on the door from my wife: "If you remain completely passive and don't come till I tell you to, I promise you a great time. Get into bed naked and await instructions." I did as my wife asked, and soon she appeared *au naturel* with a cup of warm vegetable oil. She rubbed it all over herself, then rubbed herself all over me. I became very aroused, especially when she alternated fellatio with impaling herself on my penis. But she kept insisting, "Don't come until I tell you to." Who was I to argue? After what must have been two hours, she finally gave me permission to come, and I had the most explosive orgasm of my life. Just thought you'd like to know.

—B.R., Sarasota, Florida

Thanks for sharing. You've discovered why sex experts recommend extended foreplay: It makes climaxes more climactic.

165. The One-Minute Manager

My wife and I have been together for more than eight years and have a great sex life. I love performing oral sex on her whenever she wants and almost always bring her to orgasm. But when she performs oral sex on me, it is usually just for a few minutes of foreplay and rarely to completion. The problem is not with ability—she gives great head. She just seems to get tired or loses interest after a short time. I don't take more than ten or fifteen minutes to come. Do you have any ideas that might persuade my wife to be a little more generous with her oral talents?

—D.B., San Francisco, California

It can get awfully lonely down there, especially if she's performing without feedback. Moan, groan, wriggle, talk dirty, touch her, scratch her back, lift her up and kiss her on the mouth, beg for more, go down on her at the same time, take it away from her for a few minutes, ask her to kiss your balls, or put your penis in her pussy, then back in her mouth. Then come. It's supposed to be a blow job, not a career.

166. Thrift Shop Lovers

My lover has confessed a wish to have her clothes ripped from her body, to be ravished. It occurs to me that even Hulk Hogan might have a tough time tearing a cotton T-shirt with a reinforced neck. Obviously, if the rip were started with scissors, it would be much easier. But that would destroy the moment. Any suggestions?

—K.K., Cincinnati, Ohio

Rent the movie A Clockwork Orange. *Scissors can be made to work. But the real trick is to find the right clothes. Visit a thrift shop with your lover. Stock up on older clothes that are inexpensive and worn—they'll tear more easily (especially if you run a razor down the seams beforehand). And never mind if it's not a clean rip—you can use the tatters for reins.*

167. Condom Tip

My boyfriend and I always use condoms, mainly for birth control purposes, when we have sex. But when things are hot and heavy, it disrupts the mood if he has to fumble with a rubber. Is there any way to incorporate this activity into lovemaking?

—S.A., New York, New York

Sure. You can simultaneously increase his arousal while relieving him of responsibility for suiting up. Open the package, remove the condom, and stick your tongue into the tip to remove any air. Using your lips and tongue, carefully unroll the condom to the base of his penis. To ensure a smooth fit, help it along with your hands. We think you'll both be pleased with the result.

168. Erotic Road Map

While my girlfriend was giving me a foot massage, she touched a point just behind the ball of my foot. I noticed an erotic sensation, mostly through my foot, but nonetheless very sexual. Rubbing this spot triggers sensual feelings in me, but she doesn't seem to have a corresponding spot. Any hints on where to find her erogenous zones?

—S.W., Hackensack, New Jersey

Some individuals are more sensitive to a particular stimulation than others. Spots that are usually sensitive for both sexes include the earlobes, neck, lips, nipples, inner thighs, lower back (just above the buttocks), and backs of the knees. But here's a neat exercise. Create a pleasure map to learn what spots are sensitive for your partner. Explore her body by using a scale ranging from negative to neutral to wow. See if changing the intensity of the touch changes the rating. Draw arrows or exclamation marks with a washable marker. Or leave Post-it stickers on all points of interest. Then go over your notes.

169. Making Out

My lover and I have enjoyed a loving, sensuous, and progressive relationship for the past two years. While I have had a number of lovers before, no one has ever been nearly as dynamic. When we were first nurturing this affair, before we actually engaged in intercourse, we had a number of heavy-petting sessions that left us both drained and longing for more. During one particular session, my boyfriend began massaging my nipples, bringing them to swelling points. He would roll them between his teeth and tongue, nearly driving me crazy. After no more than three or four minutes of this, I felt the beginnings of the most incredible orgasm I have ever had. However, he had not even touched me below the waist. As he kept up the pace with his tongue on my nipples, the waves broke over me, as real as if he had been using his tongue on my clitoris. I even felt the contractions that come after a particularly long and intense orgasm. Needless to say, I was blown away. Nothing like that had ever happened to me, and I was overcome with tears of relief and wonder. My lover was fairly matter-of-fact about it and acted surprised that I

had never experienced this. He had me hooked from that point on, and we have repeated this act on occasion. It's the same every time, though he has discovered that if he whispers, "Will you come for me?" it sets me off immediately. He usually waits until he has me thoroughly worked up before he pulls that trick out of his hat. My question is, Have any of your other readers experienced this before? Could it all be in my mind, or is it possible to reach a satisfying orgasm without being manually stimulated in the clitoral area?
—H.L., Sarasota, Florida

You bet. Kinsey found a woman who could reach orgasm by having her eyebrows stroked. Direct clitoral stimulation is not the only route to orgasm. The technique you describe dates back at least to the fifties, when it was known as making out, or getting to second base. There is a direct line between the nipples and the genitals—indeed, nipple stimulation is sometimes used to bring on labor in pregnant women. As a source of pleasure, it's a great way to spend a Sunday afternoon.

170. Moving Day

Sex has turned into the same old same old. Can the Advisor dig into his vast library of sex manuals and come up with some truly novel ways of making love?
—T.K., Chicago, Illinois

Lailan Young's Love Around the World *contains the following diversions for the terminally bored. We can only warn that these variations are performed by trained professionals and should not be attempted at home.*

Uplifted Woman: *This love position requires four participants, though only two enjoy themselves. The woman is held high above their heads by two attendants; she curls up her legs and the man stands on a chair or stool, if necessary. [If necessary?]*

The Balancing Act: *This is much favored by tea lovers. The man and the woman balance a bowl of tea on their heads and attempt union without spilling a drop."*

Young also cites a trick mentioned in "The Perfumed Garden": "Women of great experience, who, lying with a man, elevate one of their feet vertically in the air, and upon that foot a lamp is set full of oil, and with the wick burning. While the man is ramming them, they keep the lamp steady and burning and the oil is not spilled."

As we understand it, that's how the Great Chicago Fire started.

171. Overactive Hands

Can masturbation affect the way you have intercourse? I find that I cannot ejaculate easily inside a woman. When I am alone, I can bring myself to climax, but only after fairly active masturbation. I wonder if I have conditioned myself. What do you say?
—E.P., San Francisco, California.

An article in Sexuality Today *suggests that nonejaculation during intercourse can be linked to masturbation technique. According to Deena Andrews, a sex counselor, some men masturbate stroking themselves with such fury that their hands turn into a blur! These clients appear to have numbed their penis skin, without realizing it, through overly strenuous pumping (both in speed and grip). It is obvious that no vagina could compete with the intensity of their overly strenuous solo sex. After all, a man's hand is stronger and rougher than a vagina, so this could happen easily. Overly strenuous masturbators also tend to avoid using a lubricant (which means even more friction).*

Andrews' Rx is simple: Use a condom that is lubricated on the inside while you masturbate, so that it slips and slides, thus simulating intercourse while reducing surface friction. If you don't reach orgasm within fifteen or twenty minutes, quit and try again the next day. Don't go back to the old pattern. She also suggests exercising pubococcygeal muscles. If you are unconsciously withholding ejaculation, those are the muscles you use. By doing as many as 100 contractions a day, you will become aware of the muscles and can take control.

172. Statues

Here's a sexual technique for *Playboy* readers. My wife and I play something called statues. I call her from work and ask her to fantasize about a sexual position for lovemaking later that day. She has to find a position —anywhere in the house—and then freeze in it. I have to be able to touch her, kiss her, and eventually penetrate her without her moving a muscle. We find that the hours of planning and anticipation make great foreplay, while the challenge of finding a suitably accessible position offers both humor and tension. On different occasions, I have found her on the dining room table, on the weight bench in our home gym, or just peering out an open window, buttocks bared to the room. It is very exciting and our roles can be reversed. Sometimes I get to be the frozen one.

—E.O., Chicago, Illinois

Generations of American wives have played this game —only they called it "pretending to be asleep."

173. Multiple-Entry Warhead

I would like to make a suggestion to your male readers. One of the best moments in intercourse is penetration (I think Shere Hite found that 12 percent of the women she interviewed said it was their favorite part of sex). So why do it only once? Too many guys move from penetration to thrusting—they should try teasing us more often. I read a love manual some time ago that had some neat ideas for penetration. The author suggested taking a book of sexual positions and trying each one in front of a mirror—moving on to the next within moments of penetration. The trick is to see how many you can make it through before giving in. Another game the author suggested was a form of amateur oil wrestling. You apply baby oil to your lover's body and your own, then he tries to force himself on you. A hold occurs whenever he succeeds in penetration; all activity must stop, then he tries to pin you in a different position. Give it a try.

—M.R., New York, New York

We can't wait for oil wrestling to be an Olympic event. Thanks for the tip—or is that your line?

174. Water Works

I discovered a great way for women to masturbate. What I do is turn the water on in the tub to a comfortable temperature. Then I sit down in a reclining position, with my feet resting on the sides, and let the stream crash down and massage my clitoris. Depending on the water pressure, you may have to adjust the flow to a speed that feels good. I've been doing this for years now. I learned about multiple orgasms long before my first sexual encounter because I had experienced them under the tap. It's the best way (short of the real thing) to feel marvelous, and it leaves you clean.

—M.K., Lincoln, Nebraska

Let's hope last summer's drought doesn't repeat itself.

175. Fang Chung

I came across a book review in the local paper on a new account of the life of the Duchess of Windsor. According to the biographer, Wallis Simpson lived in China, where she "learned such exotic party tricks as lesbianism and Fang Chung, an Eastern sexual practice that purportedly can arouse even a corpse." Needless to say, since the review appeared in a family newspaper, any interesting details were omitted. What, pray tell, is Fang Chung?

—D.E., Detroit, Michigan

Isn't that the dish you serve with dim sum? No? We found the following description in Charles Higham's The Duchess of Windsor:

According to witnesses of the Chinese dossier, Wallis was taught "perverse practices" in these houses of prostitution. The practices can only mean lesbian displays and the art of Fang Chung. This skill, practiced for centuries, involved relaxation of the male partner through a prolonged and carefully modulated massage of the nipples, stomach, thighs and, after a deliberately protracted delay, the genitals. The exponent of Fang Chung was taught the nerve centers of the body so that the brushing movement of the fingers had the effect of arousing even the most moribund of men. Fang Chung was especially helpful in cases of premature ejaculation. By the application of a firm, specific touch between the urethra and the anus, climax could be delayed. Masseuses delayed intromission as long as possible to remove the fear of failure in intercourse that afflicted men suffering from dysfunction.

It's not surprising that your newspaper left this out.

176. The Condom Trick

Ribbed condoms are supposed to add to a woman's pleasure. We've been told by a woman that the ridges are annoying at best—not unlike making love to a corn cob. But let's see what their effect is on the gander. Take a ribbed condom. Turn it inside out. Those little ridges can add sensation to the male.

177. Maybe You Had to Be There

Buy a box of windup toys and set them loose on one another's naked bodies. Send a bunch of walking shoes walking toward her breast. See what effect chattering teeth have on an erect nipple.

178. The Spinner

A spinner is a time-honored Asian sexual technique given a new twist, as it were, by Wilt Chamberlain in his recent autobiography, *A View from Above*. In it, the seven-foot basketball great touts the joys of sex with women who stand less than five feet tall. According to the book, Wilt and a petite lover would have intercourse with the woman sitting on his lap. Then he would "spin them around like tops."

179. ESO

After decades of sex manuals that sought to reassure couples who were nervous about sex or to correct sexual problems, writers started to examine the basic act of sex. They were looking for ways to expand our pleasure potential, to get more bang for the buck. Alan and Donna Brauer's groundbreaking book, *ESO—Extended Sexual Orgasm*, was a catalog of techniques for increasing sexual awareness. Here are a few that you can practice by yourself:

Experiment with different kinds of strokes. Most men stimulate themselves with a basic up-and-down stroke of one hand. Some men stimulate themselves by rolling their penis in two hands. Your hand can be turned thumb up or thumb down; you can make a ring of your thumb and forefinger; you can concentrate stimulation on the shaft or the glans; you can use both hands and stroke from mid-shaft outward in both directions at once, toward the glans and toward the base; you can press your penis against your belly and rub its underside with the flat of your palm; you can change hands; and these are only a few of the many possible variations. Each time you stimulate yourself is a new experience, because you have added your previous experience to the total of what you know and feel. Your goal is not to ejaculate but to *feel more*—to enjoy the process. If you pay attention to sensation, you won't be bored. Boredom is a form of resistance.

When you have achieved hard erection and sustained it for at least five minutes, continue stroking your penis while stimulating your external prostate spot and controlling ejaculation with the scrotal-pull technique, which we will explain shortly.

Pulling your testicles away from your body prevents you from ejaculating. Try it.

To apply the scrotal pull, grasp the scrotum between your testicles with the thumb and forefinger of your left hand. When you're near orgasm, pull firmly down. At other times, for stimulation, pull lightly in rhythm as you stroke. Another way is to make a ring with your left thumb and forefinger between your testicles and body and pull downward.

As part of your self-stimulation exercises, you should practice voluntary testicle elevation and lowering. Nearing ejaculation, deliberately relax the muscles that hold your testicles close to your body and notice the effect. You may find the muscular control difficult at first, and the effect may seem too subtle to notice. Keep practicing. After the ejaculatory urge has subsided somewhat, resume stimulating your penis with your hand and at the same time deliberately elevate your testicles. Notice the subtle effect of increasing arousal.

180. Sex Secrets of Orgasmic Women

I'm at my wit's end. No matter what I try, my girlfriend does not reach orgasm through intercourse. Is it my problem?

—E.W., New York, New York

Not really. An orgasm is not something you give another person. It is something the other person shares with you. Or, to put it another way, God helps those who help themselves. The April 1984 issue of Archives of Sexual Behavior *published an interesting study on orgasmic women that supports that notion. Virtually all of the women studied said that they had "some level of conscious control over their orgasmic response" and that "they needed to participate in reaching orgasm in some meaningful way." When asked to cite the actions that facilitated their own orgasm, the women gave the following suggestions: Get into the right position (56 percent); get the right stimulation (52 percent); concentrate on sensation/good feelings (48 percent); fantasize/ visualize, including talk (44 percent); get right rhythm/speed (33 percent); concentrate on area of stimulation (30 percent); listen to partner/self for reassurance (30 percent); move with partner (30 percent); relax (30 percent); tell partner what you want (26 percent); kiss/hug (15 percent). In addition, a few women cited "decide to reach orgasm, breathe faster or deeper, flex vaginal muscles, stimulate partner, stimulate self during intercourse." (Note: In the list, "right" means what the woman thinks or knows will produce orgasm for her.) So the point is that your partner should find out what works and use it.*

181. Pumping Lust

I read with interest the letter from the Michigan girl who got turned on by giving her boyfriend a piggyback ride. I am a short, stocky girl with a very curvy body. I enjoy doing push-ups and chinning myself. The guy I am currently going with is rather small, and until recently, we had a hard time getting much pleasure out of our sexual relations. One night, when he was leaving for home, I spontaneously decided to give him a good, tight hug along with his good-night kiss, and he was so light that I just lifted him off the floor. I was immediately turned on but was worried about what he must be thinking; however, as he was pressed against me, I could feel him growing big and hard as I held him in the doorway. I nevertheless asked him if he wanted me to put him down, but he indicated that he liked it, so I turned and carried him into the bedroom. We had a very enjoyable evening, so now we always engage in a wrestling match before sexual encounters.

Our sex life has really improved since that first memorable evening, and now, whenever things get boring, I just pick him up and carry him into the bedroom for a good tussle followed by a full night of sexual delights.

—S.F., Downey, California

182. Sex Is Essentially a Form of Enthusiasm

I have been seeing a lady friend for more than a year who is very beautiful, has a great figure and, in her forties, passes for thirty. After the first few months of dating, we became intimate sexually and have continued with a very aggressive sexual program. This is all fine and I really love it, but the thing that puzzles me is that she is obsessed with fellatio. It's not that I object; she really is good at performing the act. However, I believe that if given the choice, she prefers fellatio to normal intercourse. Whenever we begin foreplay, she will go down on me immediately unless I prevent it. Then she will make the excuse that she has to put in her diaphragm, since she does not take the Pill. At times, when she is performing fellatio, she becomes very tenacious and goes at it as if she were a starving animal over its first meal. She moans and groans and makes weird noises and tries to take my entire penis into her mouth. Once she has started, there is no stopping her until I climax. She takes advantage of situations in which intercourse is not possible, such as while I am driving or in a theater, where she will insist that we sit in a remote and dark area. She fondles my penis until it is erect, then says, "I can't leave you like that," and goes down on me.

She tells me that her late husband loved fellatio and that she sucked him constantly, sometimes four or five times a day. They had no children, which is understandable. There have been evenings when we stayed at her home to watch TV. We would sit on the couch and she would make me comfortable and then lie across the couch in such a manner that she could view the TV and at the same time suck me. She has spent hours doing this, and when I have an orgasm, she becomes very aroused sexually and secretes a lot of vaginal fluids. I sometimes think that she has an orgasm herself when I do. At the completion of each orgasm, she runs her fingers down to the base of my penis and drains every drop of semen out of me, and never once has she made a spot on her or my clothes.

Now, she is definitely not a lesbian and has very little to do with women. If she were a man, you would call her a homosexual. But she is a woman and her sexual preference seems to be fellatio rather than intercourse. I am somewhat concerned: Although we have no commitments or obligations between us now, I could become serious about her. How do you describe a female—either clinically or with a slang expression—who prefers oral sex?

—S.R., Atlanta, Georgia

A real find.

183. Born-Again Virginity

What constitutes loss of virginity in a male?

—C.S., De Kalb, Illinois.

We think virginity is an outmoded concept. As Thomas Pynchon once wrote, you break your cherry on something every day. The classical definition applies to the first time you have intercourse with a female, but that is only one of the firsts. What about the first time you try oral sex or anal sex? Your first nooner? Your first time outdoors? Your first time in a crowd? The first time sex works for both of you? The first time you do it twice? The first time you do it with someone you love? The first time you do it with a complete stranger? It's a challenge: Make a list of first times and add to it.

184. Don't Yogurt That Joint

We are writing this letter to you in the hope that you will publish it in your magazine. We believe that your readers will enjoy it and may even get some good ideas from it. It all happened when our class had an orgy after a school party. We must say that it was probably the most successful orgy ever, and we know that everyone had fun. Here are some of the most interesting and erotic things that happened: (1) The first thing we did was to gather everybody (about 28 people) into the smallest room in the house. (2) For the first half hour or so, we let people do whatever they wanted, wherever they wanted to; and by the time everyone had arrived, everything was going as planned. Let the games begin! (3) When everybody had arrived, we announced that we would start the contest. Each team consisted of two people (male and female, of course) and was given a container of yogurt. Then one of the partners spread yogurt all over the other person. At the sound of the signal, the partner licked all the yogurt off. The first team to finish won a box of condoms and the second a bottle of Spanish-fly drops.

All in all, the night went very well, and nobody left alone.

—J.W.M., O.A.S., B.K., J.E.H., V.B.O., G.S.B., P.E.S., M.O., V.K.,
Norway

Why do we hear about these parties after they happen? Come on, guys. We like yogurt, too.

185. Feedback

While browsing through a recent Playboy Advisor, I came upon the letter from S.R. in Atlanta. The gentleman seems to have a deep (pun intended) concern for assigning a label to his girlfriend's propensity for fellatio. Perhaps I may offer a personal observation that will help explain why some women adore going down on their favorite man. My boyfriend has also accused me of preferring fellatio to "regular" sex—but with no complaints about the frequency. I like going down on him because my mouth is more sensitive than my vagina. I can simply feel more of what is happening with his delicious cock as he becomes more and more aroused. My hands are free to do what they will to add to the pleasure, and he is in a very comfortable and relaxing position. I become very excited knowing that he is having such a good time. The greatest part of any sex act with him is when he ejaculates. When he is cradled in my mouth, I get the full pleasure of every muscle contraction and all the sweetness of the bone, too. Since the mind is the biggest sex organ of the body, I would advise S.R. to talk with his girlfriend about her pleasure in performing fellatio. He may find that her description will be an even bigger turn-on. Then he should tell her what he likes about the things they do in bed. Forget the labels and enjoy!

—S.D., Minneapolis, Minnesota

Talking is the second-best form of oral sex. It's just hard to do with your mouth full. Thanks for the insight.

186. Riding 'Em High

My girlfriend likes to make love on top. She says that the missionary position is a sexist relic—that the male-superior position does not give women enough stimulation. Well, goddamn it, I like the power, the view, the exercise that I get when I'm on top. Can you say anything in defense of the missionary position?

—T.P., New York, New York

The missionary position has gotten a lot of bad press— a lot of it from missionaries. But there is nothing intrinsically wrong with it. Two New York–based sex researchers, Edward and Joanne Eichel, taught a group of women a sexual-alignment technique to enhance the standard missionary position. The male adopts a "riding high" position, in which his pelvis overrides the female's mons area. In addition, the couple try to grind their pubic regions together, rather than resort to the old in and out. The alignment provides constant clitoral contact. The two techniques combined give an effective twist. Almost 77 percent of the women in the research group said that they always or almost always reached orgasm in the missionary position, compared with 27 percent of females in the control group.

187. Hall of Fame

I'm writing in the hope that you can comment about my husband's sexual practices. I say they are grossly abnormal. He says he just likes "a little excitement." Please look at these examples of his style of "fun" and let me know what you think:

We were staying in a hotel and our room was several doors from a stairwell we assumed was a fire escape. We took our clothes off in our room—then went carefully out into a public hallway, past several doors, and into the stairwell, where we had sex. This was during the early evening.

Sometimes we take our clothes off in a storage room or a vacant apartment at a new complex being built, then go carefully out, down the sidewalks, and up to the edge of the occupied area, where we have sex. Then we weave our way back through the construction area to our clothes (which are sometimes several buildings away). There are numerous possibilities for us to be trapped away from our clothes. This happens both day and night.

We go out to the side of the building we live in and have sex. The area is visible from a street across a vacant lot ten yards wide. We are plainly in view of people looking in our direction from passing cars. This is in broad daylight. A policeman once saw us, but before he could make a turn and come through our parking lot to search for us, we had gotten away.

We've done such things 500 times or so over a 10-year period. My husband is thirty-five years old and I am thirty-two. We have been chased only three or four times and have been confronted three times, with only a lecture given. Sex in the privacy of our bedroom is possible. It's fun and fulfilling for both of us. So it's not that normal sex is a problem. My husband just prefers the danger. What do you say?"

—T.W., Phoenix, Arizona

If you've gotten away with this 500 times in 10 years, it strikes us that open-air sex is safer than sex in a bathtub. However, it's your perception of risk that makes the activity a problem. Tell your husband your feelings and see if you can work out a compromise.

188. Tease

I am a twenty-three-year-old graduate student currently dating an eighteen-year-old freshman whom I find to be a most erotic woman. We get into some extremely heavy petting and foreplay, including my performing some very long periods of cunnilingus. However, she doesn't totally reciprocate. Although she loves fondling and licking my cock and rubbing it between her large breasts, she refuses to bring me to orgasm. When I am ready to enter her, she refuses, saying she is a virgin and that she doesn't "do that stuff." Despite my sexual frustration, I have come to find this incredible prick-teasing extremely erotic. It has become a game of sorts, with me begging for some sort of release and her refusing, only teasing me more by stating how sexually innocent she is and at the same time fondling my organ. I know she loves being in control, having me beg for her charms. I suppose I enjoy it, too, and I have refused to relieve myself through masturbation. Instead, I find myself with a constant hard-on. I recently persuaded her, with much pleading, to give me a hand job. With some reluctance, she relented, and with her lovely hands and nails, I had the best orgasm of my life; in fact, I nearly passed out with pleasure!

Is this situation totally unusual? I have never heard of a man enjoying being teased so much. Is there something wrong with me or my girlfriend? We both seem to enjoy this role-playing so much. If we ever do have intercourse, do you think we will lose a certain thrill in our relationship?

I love her so much but am beginning to question my sexual role.

—G.C., Knoxville, Tennessee

So what's the problem? Many men enjoy extended foreplay, and it could just be that you enjoy this woman's company—not to mention her touch—so much that coitus is secondary to you. We see nothing wrong or all that unusual; if it works for the two of you, fine.

189. Doggie-Style Debate

Your informative response to the following question, which has been bothering me for quite some time, would be sincerely appreciated. While making love in the "doggie-style" position, which way is more pleasurable—with the woman's legs outside the man's legs or with her legs between the man's legs? I know that you may think this is a dumb question, but I enjoy that position very much and would like to know which way is better. In adult movies, you see the performers doing it most often with the woman's legs between the man's, and unfortunately, the only way I have tried it is with my legs outside the man's.

—G.M., San Diego, California

The point of adult movies is not always pleasure but, rather, a pleasurable image. Putting the woman's legs outside the man's legs would block the camera angle. As to which position is better: It depends on your goal. The legs-inside position does increase the friction and indirectly stimulates the clitoris. And you know where that leads: astonishing orgasms (especially for the female). The legs-outside position allows greater depth and possibly a better view. And you know where that leads: astonishing orgasms (more likely for the male). Our advice: Flip a coin. Tails wins.

190. Oral History

My boyfriend and I had an exciting experience while I was giving him head, and I'd like to tell you about it so you can explain why it happened. On the evening in question, I had decided to eat my boyfriend and take my time doing so, as he was slightly hornier than usual. While I was enjoying myself eating him, I would pull and suck gently on the head of his penis on the upstroke. Often I would rub my tongue in tiny twirling circles on the tip. I could feel him readying for orgasm. As he got beyond the point of resisting, I ceased the oral stimulation so I could feel him squirt his come into my mouth. I noticed that his orgasm was not as powerful as usual. I had just enough time to swallow once when he grabbed my head. It was obvious that he needed more oral stimulation, so I quickly resumed it. I could feel him growing harder; I knew he was going to have another orgasm; and when he did, I got quite a mouthful—I had to swallow while he was still coming. He was exhausted; I was surprised and excited, as I had always wanted to return the favor of multiple orgasm to him. I didn't think it was possible, so I had never bothered to try. Now that I did it, I don't know how to do it again. We do have a theory: That it may have happened because I ceased stimulation just before he came. We will try out our theory, but we would greatly appreciate any information or suggestions you might have on the matter. I love making him feel good, and this is almost as good as what he does to me.

—J.M.D., Detroit, Michigan

Ejaculation and orgasm are not necessarily simultaneous in men, and what may have happened in the situation you describe was your partner's ejaculating before he actually climaxed. Then, shortly thereafter, he had a full orgasm and ejaculated again. This is one of those delightful experiences that happen under ideal circumstances—with the right partner, perhaps after extended foreplay, and maybe (but not necessarily) following a fairly lengthy period since the previous orgasm. There is no way to guarantee that this will occur on a regular basis, or even to know whether or not it will happen again, but the two of you should have a lot of fun trying.

191. Pregnant Play

Here's what we do: After foreplay, when I'm turned on and moistly ready, my husband and I both lie on our backs. He scoops one arm under my back and pulls me partially on top of him, my back next to his chest, while I cuddle him close with my arm around his shoulders. Turning my body at a slight angle to his, I reach down and help him slip inside me from beneath. He's able to fondle my breasts with his free hand, and our mouths can meet in a deep, exciting kiss. (He can also bury his face in the breast closer to him, which he finds very stimulating.) My favorite part in all this is that by being face-up with him inside me, I have easy access to my most sensitive region and can manually bring myself to a satisfying climax. My husband sometimes pulls me directly on top of him, and says he loves running his hands up and down my breasts and stomach as he reaches his own orgasm. This may sound like a gymnastics exercise, but it's really fun and comfortable once you've tried it a few times. We highly recommend it and hope this suggestion will help other pregnant couples enjoy lovemaking at a time when it otherwise might be very uncomfortable.

—J.S., Los Angeles, California

192. Ben-wa Balls

Recently, one of my lovers gave me a pair of ben-wa balls, which I had wanted for a long time. One of the balls is hollow, the other filled with liquid. The woman inserts the two spheres into her vagina, and the constant clacking together is supposed to leave her in a state of ecstasy, or at least continual arousal. I was quite excited by the idea, so as soon as he gave them to me, I inserted them. We were out and about, and as I walked down the street, I could feel one slipping out. Fortunately, there was a hotel nearby and I was able to duck into the bathroom before it fell onto the sidewalk (which might have marred its gold-plated finish). Anyway, I am having the damnedest time keeping them in, and when they do stay in, I don't notice. I was expecting a continuous turn-on, even looking forward to wearing them to the office. So what am I doing wrong? And can they harm me in any way or cut down on my sensitivity during "normal" lovemaking? Please explain what they are supposed to do.

—L.G., Berkeley, California

Ben-wa balls are a safety hazard, no doubt. The damned things fall out at the oddest times. Many's the time we've spied a golden sphere ricocheting down the escalator at the local shopping mall. It's always a minor scene: "Excuse me, miss . . ." Supposedly, the vibrations of the balls' clicking together will drive a woman to erotic frenzy. Guess again. Probably the only use for the little buggers is to exercise the pubococcygeus muscle—i.e., the clenching needed to keep them in is a great move during lovemaking. You might consider one of the modern variants of ben-wa balls. Most erotic boutiques sell egg-shaped vibrators with remote-control devices. You slip the egg into your underwear, twist the dial, and presto: a great way to ease the daily commute.

193. Taste Technique

My wife and I have a fantastic love life. We are in our early forties, have been married more than twenty years, and enjoy sex on an average of once a day. What is the problem? My semen smells and tastes like bleach. (I know from secondhand knowledge that it has a bitter taste.) Although my wife loves to give head, I can understand her reluctance to take a mouthful of bleach. Can you suggest a way, through either diet or some other method, that I can improve the taste of my semen?

—R.W.B., Rapid City, South Dakota

It is difficult, if not impossible, to alter the taste of semen. However, your wife can try a few techniques to minimize her distaste, including gargling with a pleasant-tasting mouthwash while indulging in fellatio and positioning the penis farther back in the mouth to bypass the taste buds. But we still have one question about this letter that really bothers us: How do you know what bleach tastes like? Are people out there chugging Clorox?

194. The Good-bye Kiss

Over the past year or so, I've noticed in your magazine several references to a style of fellatio that for want of a better name could be called the good-bye kiss. In Susan Squire's article on oral sex, it is suggested that women perform oral sex just as their boyfriends are leaving the house. The notion is that this will drain them of desire and give them something to think about. Does this really work? If I go down on my boyfriend when he goes to work, will it keep him from fooling around?

—D.S., New York, New York

Yes. You have our word on it. You might also try performing oral sex when he leaves the room, or for that matter, when he tries to get up from the dining room table. Do you believe us? Oh, well, it was worth a try. As near as we can tell, an entire generation of women grew up with that bit of advice. The message is not being passed along. It gives us pause: Is it possible that the best oral sex of the century is already a thing of the past?

195. Kegel Kreativity

Are Kegel exercises really effective? Almost every book of sex advice for women tells them to practice clenching and releasing their vaginal muscles. What do you think?

—R.O., Bloomington, Indiana

We can't wait for our health club to put in a Nautilus machine that exercises the pubococcygeal muscle. Now, that would be interesting. There is new evidence in support of Kegel exercises. A study at the State University of New York at Stony Brook measured vaginal pulses in three groups of women. Women who tensed their vaginal muscles showed greater degrees of arousal than women who simply fantasized about sex. But, to show that sex is not just a body experience, the study found that women who fantasized and contracted their vaginal muscles had the greatest degree of arousal.

196. Cheerleader Sex

Please tell me if the following is a rarity or if you've come across this type of obsession before. My girlfriend, who's twenty-two, and I, twenty-four, like to watch sex films a lot when we're warming up to make love. Lately, we have both expressed an interest in viewing films of cheerleaders doing kicks and bending over to show off their asses. We admitted this to each other while watching a recent basketball game during which the cameraman was shooting a tight close-up of a cheerleader's skirt as she was doing a kick. The sight turned me on, so I jokingly said, "Oh, what a pretty sight!" To my surprise, my girlfriend said, "I agree!" This led to a heavy bout of lovemaking, during which she put on her high school cheerleader's outfit and told me about the affair she had had with one of her fellow cheerleaders in the eleventh grade. More surprising, it had been with one of our closest friends, an absolutely beautiful brown-haired, brown-eyed female, definitely the very epitome of femininity—aside from my girlfriend, of course! The girl is still single, and we are thinking of asking her about having a threesome. (My girlfriend has also confessed that while they made out, they both wore their cheerleader's skirts and panties, pulling the crotch to the side to have access to each other.) Anyway, the reason I am writing is to see if you can locate for us a distributor of videos that feature pretty women dressed as cheerleaders, doing what cheerleaders normally do: kicking and bending over, showing off their pretty butts. The photos should be taken close to the women's crotches, too. We are also interested in magazines of this type. I have written to every video and magazine outlet I can find and have found nothing of this type.

—J.C., Rutherfordton, North Carolina

Sometimes we think that America is turning sex into a spectator sport. Whatever happened to do-it-yourself ingenuity? Buy a Polaroid or, even better, rent a video camera and recorder. Invite your girlfriend's friend over for a photo session. Have them dress up in their old duds and see what happens.

197. An Ad for Caller ID

This story isn't like most stories dealing with sexual problems, unusual sexual appetites, or chance meetings between the sexes. It's about an erotic, incredibly horny woman who calls me once a week from 3,000 miles away in order to satisfy her sex drive. The mystifying thing about this relationship is that I don't know who she is. It all started back East about six years ago, when she spotted me going home from my bank teller's job. As she called me that first time and told me all the things she wanted us to do to each other, I became intrigued that she knew all about me. I did not hear from her after that.

So here I was living in Los Angeles, almost two years later. The phone rang and this familiar voice said, "Recognize this voice?" I almost died. She called regularly after that, describing in detail the many sexual habits she enjoys—taking on two guys at once, doing it with another woman, taking my cock down her throat. I must say that I look forward to her phone calls. We often talk of meeting one day. She loves to get me going and moans and groans while I'm describing my tongue in her pussy and her mouth on my dick. To be honest, I hope this never ends. This fantasy keeps me going on the slow days. I know other guys pay to hear these words. I feel lucky to have her calling me—and picking up the tab.

—C.F.P., Glendale, California

198. Office Break

I have just discovered a good, indecent way for women to refresh themselves at the office on a stressful day. I am still quaking with excitement over this rest room technique. Let me describe it: In a stall (with a door, unless you're an outrageous or crude exhibitionist), note whether or not the toilet paper holder is reflective, preferably boxlike (the kind with the horrible tiny sheets). If it is not, somehow prop up a mirror on the inside so that when you lean back against the opposite wall and use your thigh muscles to squat a bit, you can (gosh!) see yourself! Not a brand-new sight but wildly fun if you're reasonably sure no one's going to rush after you to meet your deadline or reasonably sure you can proceed without making a tremendous commotion. I found taking as many clothes off as possible breathtakingly brave. I also found that once the friendly interplay between hand and you-know-what got going, I was in ecstasy in seconds. The quickest picker-upper ever! And harmless, too; but watch out for your lustful boss(es), or else you may be in double trouble up to your asses.

—S.W., Washington, D.C.

If it improves employee morale, what the hell. Now if we can only find someone to type this.

199. Tricks Not to Try

Have you heard of a sexual practice called gerbil stuffing? I've heard rumors that certain celebrities have had to go to emergency rooms for removal of cuddly house pets from their private parts. I know this sounds disgusting, but could it possibly be true?

—T.B., Boston, Massachusetts

Every few years, the collective unconscious goes bonkers and delivers a rumor such as this. A few years ago, it was the one about the lady who dried her kitten in the microwave oven. Last year, it was about wrapping hamsters in duct tape, so they won't explode when you fuck them. This year, it's about gerbil stuffing. The Friend of a Friend Network claims that homosexuals and/or extremely strange heterosexuals are inserting manicured gerbils into their rectums. A squirming rodent is not our idea of sexual ecstasy. We don't know how popular the practice is (have you seen anyone farting fur?), but the rumor is rampant. While we are sure that there are people out there stupid enough to try this (medical literature is filled with reports of people who have had to have removed such objects as a turnip, a toothbrush holder, a water glass, a lightbulb, soft-drink bot-

tles, a steer's horn, cucumbers, apples, hard-boiled eggs, broom handles, soldering irons, bananas, salamis, carrots, whip handles, test tubes, baseballs, flashlights, grindstones and frozen pigs' tails), obviously none of them read the Playboy Advisor.

200. Sharing Fantasies

My husband and I have been married for more than fifteen years. About five years ago, my husband confessed to me that all those years, whenever he made love to me, he had had this fantastic "moving picture" in his mind—of me and a former lover both naked, locked in sexual embrace, and enjoying it. He described, in detail, this fantastic sexual act. Needless to say, this commentary excited me very much, which in turn excited my husband even more. Since that day, we have been having sexual fantasies involving me and my lover, and we have built around them the most fabulous sex life. Now the mere mention of my lover's name by my husband acts like a mantra to me. I get sexually aroused immediately, and this excites my husband. The more I talk about it and the more details I mention, the better he likes it. Similarly, the more detail with which my husband describes my sexual encounter with my lover, the more excited I become. We are very much in love; we have never had any extramarital affairs. I eagerly wait to hear your comments and those of your readers. Is this behavior in any way strange? Has any other reader experienced anything like this?

—C.H., Long Beach, California

We get several letters a month from people who engage in this kind of aural sex. It's the adult version of an imaginary playmate, a way to introduce a touch of the strange into a healthy relationship.

201. Will It Come When You Call?

I'm currently dating a wonderful woman who has one troubling tendency: She has given my penis a pet name. Is this some kind of psychological problem? Is she immature? Have you ever heard of nicknames for private parts?

—F.D., Portland, Oregon

Actually, it's quite common to use pet names. Who speaks Latin in bed? "I'd like to linguate your labia majora" doesn't have quite the ring of "Let me lick you all over for a quarter—please, baby, please, baby." Researcher Martha Cornog analyzed pet names for private parts and came up with five typical categories. Some 6 percent of the pet names were variations of the owner's name (e.g., Little Willy for the penis of a guy named Bill). Fifty-one percent of the respondents used some other person's name or other designation (such as Little Guy for the penis and Myra and Myrtle for breasts). Some 11 percent used a descriptive word or phrase (such as Gnarled Tree Trunk for a heavily veined penis or Sweet Pea for the clitoris). Almost a third (32 percent) used a humorous or metaphorical allusion (such as Omar the Tentmaker for an erect penis or Ping and Pong for testicles). About 11 percent simply used another word.

(There was some overlap between categories.) Cornog points out that as a rule, sexual parts are the only body parts people give nicknames to. (We do know one guy who tattooed his toes LEFT *and* RIGHT, *but he doesn't know his ass from his elbow. He calls his penis the Throbbing Python of Love.) So relax and enjoy the conversation. Anything that breaks the sexual ice is okay, as long as your penis answers when it's called.*

202. Plucked Penis

I have discovered a way to increase the pleasure of sex for both the man and the woman. It involves a bit of discomfort for the man but makes a significant difference in his stamina and in the intensity of pleasure experienced by both partners. It may seem odd at first, but, speaking from experience, I know it works. My lover and I greatly enjoy sex, and we make love as often as we are able. After a marathon session one night, I became quite uncomfortable. The constant friction of pubic hair against my penis had caused me to become very sore, and it made my lover sore, too. Checking myself closely, I realized that my pubic hair grew rather densely at the base of my penis and even grew all the way up the shaft. The next day, after my shower, I used my tweezers and began plucking out those hairs on the shaft, one by one. I must say that there is nothing erotic or pleasant about this; but when I was finished, there wasn't a hair to be found on the shaft. I used a good lotion for a couple of days to soothe the soreness. The result is that the soft, smooth skin of my penis gives and receives much more stimulation inside my lover's vagina. It is an entirely new experience. She also enjoys fellatio even more, since she doesn't have to take any hair into her mouth. A bonus that most men don't think about is that it is possible to make a penis look better. Plucking the hair from the shaft and trimming the pubic area spruces things up a bit and actually makes the penis look larger. I just want to pass this information to others, as I think everyone should take some responsibility for satisfying his or her lover.

—P.P., Dallas, Texas

203. Giddyap

Can you tell me if my girlfriend is normal? The first time we made love, we were lying on a couch. Long before we had undressed, she was straddling my knee and rubbing her crotch in a rhythmic fashion, obviously in an effort to get aroused. She continued to do this throughout the evening. I would penetrate, we would reach orgasm, and then she would continue to rock her pelvis against my thigh. It certainly seemed to keep her in the mood, but I wonder if you've ever seen or heard of this before.

—M.P., Chicago, Illinois

We first heard about this in Xaviera Hollander's Super-sex. *The knee ride mimics a form of masturbation that many young girls practice—they rub against a pillow or an arm of a sofa. (Later, they graduate to horseback riding, but that's another story.) What works when they're young still works as they grow older. Women who have trouble reaching orgasm during intercourse often resort to this method—*

it allows them to rock back and forth in a familiar rhythm, without wasting an erection (their partners may find that rhythm too exciting to withhold their own orgasms). Finally, this form of nonpenetration is making a comeback as a form of safe sex between heterosexuals concerned about birth control and/or venereal disease. The woman can masturbate the man and/or hold on for dear life when the ride gets wild, without worry.

204. Change

Like many guys, I used to have a problem with premature ejaculation—a few thrusts and I would reach orgasm. I started looking for ways to prolong sex and, much to my surprise, I've discovered one. Watching porn movies, I've noticed that the participants never have sex in just one position. They start with oral sex; then he turns her over and enters from the rear; then she sits on top; then she turns and faces the other way, and so forth. At first I thought they were doing it to change the camera angles and make the film interesting. But I tried it and found that by breaking concentration and changing positions, I was able to last a lot longer. My partner views it as teasing. Sometimes I just rub the tip of my penis against her clitoris; sometimes she touches herself to maintain a rhythm for herself. When she looks ready to come, I get serious. The added benefit is that if I prolong the preliminaries, I seem to maintain my erection longer after one orgasm, and it's easier to get a second.

—F.W., Philadelphia, Pennsylvania

It sounds like good advice to us: Orgasm in a male is usually the result of rhythmic stroking action. If you make love in one position, any thrusting leads to a sense of inevitability. Anything you do to break the rhythm will put off the orgasm. This is not close-order drill. We once read about a cure for premature ejaculation that may explain why this tactic works: "Since quick orgasm is an exclusively male problem, avoid it by pretending that you aren't male. Be a tease instead. Forget about total penetration and adopt the characteristics of the coy female virgin. Do all the things she would do: Be bold, then be frightened; go forward, then retreat; be capricious, indecisive and seemingly unsure of whether you actually intend to go through with it or not." In short, play.

205. The Good-Night Caress

Some time ago, I had a date with an attractive young thing who had an ironclad rule about how far to go in a first encounter. The chemistry was right, and after an evening of heavy petting, we were both experiencing a lot of sexual tension. When it was time to say good night, I decided there was no reason for both of us to go to bed horny, so I enhanced the good-night kiss by masturbating her with the palm of my hand through her clothing. My little courtesy surprised and thrilled her—no one had ever done it for her before, she said—and our next date resulted in some wild and uninhibited sack time. While I have used this dry-masturbation technique before, when sex was impossible for some reason or another, I have never masturbated an undressed female. In fact, I'm not sure exactly how to go about it properly. Since there are a number of delightful things to do in the sack that could be enhanced by manual stimulation of the female genitalia, it might be useful if the Advisor would give all of us clumsy male readers some basic instruction in this delicate area.

—J.J., Newport Beach, California

Ask your unclad friend to show you how she masturbates. Or have her touch an area of your body to give signals (faster, slower, softer, right or left, up and down, whatever). Then, for variety, try feathers, fur mittens, silk scarves, or gasoline-powered vibrators for a sensation that she is not used to. Use your toes under the table. This list should get you through your next date.

206. The Interlocking Venus Butterfly

I am happy to inform you that I am the inventor of the Venus Butterfly, though how *L.A. Law* found out about it, I haven't the foggiest idea. Enclosed please find drawings of the maneuver, for maneuver it is—not an insect implement or a biological part. The thumbs, side by side, support the chin, since, as I'm sure you've found, the neck gets tired while you're performing lengthy cunnilingus. The forefingers are used to spread the labia; the joined middle fingers are inserted into the vagina, and the ring fingers are interlocked.

Well, folks, there you have it. I do claim royalties

every time the Venus Butterfly is used. Let's see . . .
what's your circulation?

—E.C.C. Jr., Dover, New Hampshire

207. Dear John

Back in the early seventies, I had gotten Dear Johned
by my high school sweetheart when I had just a few
weeks left in Vietnam. Despondent and depressed, I
found myself in a massage parlor being worked over by
a very lovely Oriental lady. Noticing how unhappy I was
she inquired in broken English as to what was wrong.
After I had explained the situation to her, she said that
if I came back the next day with ten dollars, she would
teach me how to make love to a woman so well that
whomever I picked up would never leave me. Not only
did I go back the next day, I went back the next ten. It
was the best $100 I've ever invested. On the third day, I
learned about the Venus Butterfly. It really exists and is
as follows: While the lady lies on her back, you place
her right leg over your shoulder, allowing your face
easy access to her pubic mound. With tender, gentle
movements, spread her pussy lips apart with your left
hand, exposing the clit and forming the shape of a
butterfly. While flicking and gently darting your tongue
on and around the clit, sometimes sucking gently upon
it, slowly and gently open and close the lips upon the
clit with your left index finger and thumb, much like a
butterfly flapping its wings. Develop a rhythm, as this
will also massage the clit. At the same time, for added
pleasure, move the thumb of your right hand in and out

of the vagina. This also gives your partner something to bear down upon as she orgasms.

—N.E.K., Scranton, Pennsylvania

208. Three-in-One Condom Trick

I am worried about contracting a venereal disease during sex. What should I do? Also, I suffer from premature ejaculation. Any suggestions? And finally, I would like to increase the size of my penis. What do you recommend?

—J.W., New York, New York

Here are the answers to your queries: (1) Wear a condom. (2) Wear two condoms. (3) Wear three condoms.

209. The Flexible Flyer

There's a girl in my aerobics class who is incredibly limber. We've become lovers and already we've exhausted most of the known positions. We're trying to figure out ways to make love that will tap her flexibility. Any suggestions?

—S.C., Boston, Massachusetts

We think it's time you took a tour of India and tried some of the positions you see in temple carvings—or read a few of those ancient sex manuals. The Perfumed Garden, for example, describes the following: "The woman must wear a pair of pantaloons, which she lets drop upon her heels;

then she stoops, placing her head between her feet, so that her neck is in the opening of her pantaloons. At that moment, the man, seizing her legs, turns her upon her back, making her perform a somersault; then, with his legs curved under him, he brings his member right against her vulva and, slipping it between her legs, inserts it. It is alleged that there are women who, while lying on their backs, can place their feet behind their heads without the help of pantaloons or hands." If you can't find a pair of pantaloons, tights will do nicely.

210. How to Write Dirty

My girlfriend goes to a school in another state. One of the ways we keep this long-distance affair going is by exchanging sex fantasies by mail. We've read Anaïs Nin's and Lonnie Barbach's collections of sexual fantasies, as well as the books by Nancy Friday. We then try to custom-tailor fantasies for each other. Neat, right? Now, here is the problem, if it is a problem: We've noticed that my fantasies are longer and more varied than hers. Does this bode ill for the relationship? I've read that different levels of desire in a couple can wreak havoc. Are different fantasies an early warning?
—P.J., Boston, Massachusetts

Relax. If you are uninhibited enough to share fantasies, this relationship has a great chance of making it into the Playboy Advisor Hall of Fame. Don't let distance be the only excuse for sharing X-rated scenarios; be sure to keep it up when you're next to each other. It happens that the differences you've noticed are normal. Two researchers at the

University of South Carolina asked students to write sexual fantasies. As a rule, males wrote longer, more explicit and varied fantasies than did females. When researchers showed subjects different types of fantasies first, the homework changed. Males, when they read fantasies involving sexual activity with relationships, mentioned more specific sex organs than did males reading examples involving casual strangers. Females included more sex organs when they read examples describing sexual encounters between casual strangers than when they read fantasies describing sex within a relationship. You figure it out. Not surprisingly, the level of guilt that a participant experienced affected the length of the fantasy he or she wrote. When a person is uptight, his or her fantasies are shorter and show less variety. And people who feel guilty are less aroused by the fantasies they read or write. But listen—being totally without guilt and terminally horny, we enjoy a good fantasy, too. Next time you write, send us a fantasy. Maybe we'll publish it.

211. Bondage Basics

My girlfriend has confided in me that one of her fantasies is to be restrained with white silk ties to a four-poster while I make love to her in a variety of ways. And, like any gentleman, I am eager to accommodate the lady. My question is, What are the rules of etiquette regarding lashing one's lady friend to the bedposts? Do you start with the arms or the legs? Most important, what kind of knots do you recommend? Single loops or doubles?
—A.K., Toronto, Ontario

Have you checked out Alex Comfort's landmark love manual, The Joy of Sex? *There are more pages on knot-tying in it than there are in the Boy Scout handbook. Comfort made soft bondage an accepted fantasy. This is a personal matter between you and your lady friend, and your imagination should be the only limit. However, it's always good to have rules when engaging in bondage, including a clearly understood code or signal to stop when either partner is truly uncomfortable or does not want to continue. Beyond that, however, you're on your own. It makes sense to us, though, to first tie the hands/arms of your submissive partner to add to the fantasy of immediate helplessness. As for knots, again, it's a matter of preference—but if you're using silk ties and hope to wear them again, you'll go easy on the loops. Don't tie any knots so tight as to impair circulation. Let your lover help you by telling you what she does and doesn't like. After all, it's her fantasy.*

212. The Car Wash

My lover and I like to find ways of turning household chores into sexual encounters. If you have to clean a bathroom, start naked. Or wear a French maid's outfit. Those are pretty obvious. The one chore whose sexual potential eluded us was washing the car. You have some of the elements—suds, the wet T-shirt contest appeal of getting soaked through and through. The only problem was the temperature of the water. Cold water can be a turnoff. We solved the problem by running the hose down to the basement laundry and using warm water. I pushed my girlfriend down on the hood of the car, thrust the hose into her cutoffs, and watched water pressure do its work. She slipped soapy hands into my shorts to return the favor. Of course, you still have to clean the car, but what the heck.

—O.S., the Internet

213. High-Heeled Sneakers

My husband has a thing about high-heeled shoes. He expects me to wear them everywhere we go. He also likes to masturbate while I walk around and/or step on things in them. He claims that most men get off on high heels to some extent, and I guess I do notice men staring at my shoes once in a while. Although my husband does dwell on them too much sometimes, we still have normal sex regularly. I like to please him, but sometimes it seems as if it's all he has on his mind, and it can get annoying. Is he sick? Do a lot of men like high heels, and why? Are there any books that refer to high-heel fetishes?

—S.F., Detroit, Michigan

Your husband may be a bit kinky, but he's not necessarily abnormal. A lot of men have a certain fascination with high heels on women. Just look through your back issues of Playboy—*half of our photographers wouldn't be able to focus a camera if there weren't a pair of high heels in the picture. Your high heels provide an extra sexual stimulus for your husband, and as long as you don't mind indulging him once in a while, there's really no problem.*

214. The Chrome Trailer Hitch

My boyfriend can come inside me and while masturbating, but he can't come when I give him head. I know there is nothing wrong with him physically, and my mouth is in great shape (I've had plenty of experience and it has never failed me before). He wants very badly to come in my mouth, and I would love it if he could. Do you have any suggestions?

—K.C., Milwaukee, Wisconsin

Chances are that your problem stems primarily from a lack of sufficient friction. We think that you and your boyfriend should experiment with different positions, and you —and he—should use more manual stimulation during fellatio to help him reach orgasm. Oral sex is loving *hand to mouth. Pick up the tempo. Shift gears. Suck the chrome off a trailer hitch. Add outside stimulation: position a mirror so that he can see you. Do it in unexpected spots—elevators and parking garages—or at unexpected times. Wake him up with oral sex.*

215. Sensual Safe Sex

All of this talk about safe sex leaves me cold. The clinical alternatives sound like making love in one of those radioactive laboratory setups, with your partner on the other side of a glass screen, your hands in some robot-powered gloves, and then a shower afterward for decontamination. Can you put some fun back into my love life?

—P.J., Columbus, Ohio

The Boston Phoenix *published a special safe sex kit that included a menu of low-risk erotic activities. For light fare, it suggested*

> *talking to each other about safer sex. Kissing and hugging. Back rubs, foot rubs and body rubs while still partially dressed. Listening to music and/or dancing together. Playing strip poker, strip backgammon or spin the bottle. Stroking, brushing or playing with each other's hair. Caressing, tickling, pinching and nibbling each other through clothes. Reading erotic literature together. Looking at erotic pictures. Watching erotic movies on the VCR. Talking sexy or sharing fantasies. Dry humping. Undressing each other or watching each other undress. Dressing up in erotic lingerie or costumes. Showering together. Kissing or licking or fondling your partner's body (except for the genitals and anus). Rubbing any non-petroleum-based body oil or lotion on each other or yourself. Putting a condom on your partner.*

For entrees, the paper suggested

> *petting with no clothes on. Stroking, caressing and fondling your partner's body (including the genitals and anus). Mutual or simultaneous masturbation to orgasm with your hands (with or without condoms, with no exchange of semen or vaginal fluids). Mutual or simultaneous masturbation with a vibrator (no sharing!). Rubbing your penis against healthy, unbroken skin on your partner's body between the breasts, between the lower thighs or against the buttocks, making sure not to ejacu-*

late in or on your partner's body orifices. Rubbing your vulva against healthy, unbroken skin on your partner's body orifices. Oral sex (fellatio) while wearing a condom. Oral sex (cunnilingus) while using a rubber dam or plastic wrap. Vaginal intercourse with a condom. Anal intercourse with a condom. Vaginal or anal penetration with a sex toy (no sharing!).

For dessert, if you still have any energy left:

Licking whipped cream or flavored non-petroleum-based oil off your partner's body, except for unprotected body openings. Masturbating while your partner watches or holds you. Making sexy video tapes or playing with a Polaroid camera. Body painting with non-petroleum-based body paints. Holding each other. Talking to each other. Sleeping together. Eating breakfast, lunch or dinner in bed. Starting over.

These are good suggestions whether or not you are worried about contracting AIDS.

216. Another Flexible Flyer

In response to the letter from S.C. in Boston, my gal is also very flexible, and we've devised some interesting positions. (1) Have your girlfriend lie flat on her back on the floor; bringing her legs and hips upward and over, she should be able to touch her knees to the floor by her head. In this position, you should be able to enter her, with the added pleasure of her having a ringside view of the action. (2) You'll need two chairs and two lengths of rope (length determined by your girlfriend's ability to do a split). Tie the legs of the chairs together so they cannot move beyond the split she will be doing on them. Have her face you as you lie flat on the floor. She should do some splits on the floor to limber up and then do them on the chairs; you reach up and help her bounce down to your waiting hard-on. It takes a little practice, and be careful not to pull any muscles.

—E.J., Cedar Rapids, Iowa

Gee. It's time to renew that membership in our health club. Your suggestions stretch more than the imagination. Try lying down beneath her to perform oral sex (you'd be going up on her). Then she can watch you masturbate, or can reach down one hand to help.

217. The Thrill of the Chaise

Let me offer this as a piece of advice, for what it is worth. I had been trying to get onto a lovely red-haired girl for many a moon, taking her to dinner and such, but she had continued to demur. Finally—I don't know how the idea suddenly came into my head—when we were at the beach, I suggested that she look under the chaise longue on which I was lying facedown, to see what she could find. The supportive fabric of the thing consisted of tough transverse plastic straps that were separated enough for me to put something through. As it happened, it was partially draped with a big beach towel, cutting off the view of the underside from people a few paces farther down the beach. The girl blushed to her ear rims delightedly, as only a redhead can do, and plunged under there with the enthusiasm of a keen auto mechanic going under a fine racecar. I went back to pretending to read my *War and Peace*, miming an intent and focused concentration and trying, very soon, not to moan. I had never before realized how deeply a girl could take a penis in her mouth. She told me that what broke the dam, so to speak, was the exciting prospect of bringing it off surreptitiously in public and, at the same time, more or less having a man, in a sweet way, at her mercy. I have seen cartoons, of course, involving girls administering blow jobs under well-curtained restaurant tables, but this seaside approach had never before occurred to me. It is an excellent way of reaching an accord between masculine desires and the fantasies of many women. And accord, rather than exploitation, is a pleasure in sex I like.

—J.W., Manchester, Connecticut

War and Peace *has always worked for us.*

218. The Hovering Butterfly

A few years ago, while I was researching some ancient Taoist texts at a famous library in England, I came across a few volumes on the tao of sex. In one written during the Tang dynasty (A.D. 618–907), I found the sexual technique called the Hovering Butterfly. In this technique, the man lies on his back, with both legs open but drawn toward his chest. The woman sits astride him with the penis inserted. Once the penis is firmly entrenched, the man clamps his legs on the woman's waist. Then she moves up and down, which causes his legs to move in such a way as to resemble the flapping and hovering butterfly. (In this position, the woman can also lean forward and the man can suck her breasts at will.) The woman has to be quite agile. She should have good vaginal muscle control. She has to use her vaginal muscles to milk the penis to get the man to ejaculate, because in this position, he cannot penetrate too deeply with ease. A woman who can master vaginal control is the ultimate coitus queen and is worth more than gold. The best way to utilize this technique is to alternate letting the woman ride up and down for a while with letting her sit still but use her vaginal muscle control. The last piece of advice is that the couple should take care while the woman is moving, for the penis may easily slip out if its penetration is not deep enough.

—T.H., Copenhagen, Denmark

219. The Marble Peach

Along with everybody else in America, I read *Presumed Innocent*, the heralded potboiler by Scott Turow. I was mesmerized by the following passage: "She bumped her behind against me until I realized that what I was being offered, was a marble peach." Marble peach? Is this a new colloquialism for anal intercourse?

—B.Z., Chicago, Illinois

We asked Turow, who is a Chicago attorney as well as a hugely successful first novelist, about the marble peach in question. Indeed, he coined the phrase, which we must ad-

mit we like enormously. "It was simply a metaphor," Turow told us. "Now it seems to have taken on cult significance. One morning last summer, I was getting off my train at Union Station and I noticed a guy in business attire approaching me with a smile. As he drew closer, he said sort of surreptitiously, 'Don't say anything—just listen. Marble peach! Baskin-Robbins' flavor of the month.' "

220. Hair

Lately, I've been hearing a lot of talk about the average woman's alleged inability to achieve orgasm during intercourse. It seems that due to the poor location of the clitoris, so far away from the vagina, there's just no way to stimulate it, short of just reaching down there and rubbing that little bugger with those dishpan-callused mitts—right, guys? Wrong, guys. Evidently, Whoever created these wonderful bodies in which we take so much pride also had our partners' pleasure in mind, for what did He (She, It) place on our bodies in the same area? Hair, you fools! Any woman will tell you (if you'd bother to ask) that the clitoris is something to be handled gently, even tenderly! Fingers, if they're not clean, soft, and manicured, might as well be stuck up your own ass, where they're out of the way. Hair, boys! It's there; use it. For starters, put away your harsh soap. You wouldn't use that stuff on your head, would you? Get out your good shampoo and the best conditioner you can find. Avoid the ones that use waxes for sheen and look for a pH of 4.5 to 5.5. Check with the local beauty parlor or whoever cuts your hair for brand names. Work with the stuff until your hair is nice and soft and healthy.

Next comes the technique. Not a whole lot to it, really. I'd think more people would have thought of it, but I guess there's no underestimating the average American male. To start, assume your standard missionary position; then, once you're inserted, bring your lady's legs up alongside your torso. Now, instead of your normal in-and-out thrusting, try this: For the outstroke, instead of pulling back away from her, let your hips slide down toward her ass. This accomplishes two things: It keeps your body directly against hers for stimulation on the instroke and it aligns your member at a slightly angled-up position. Now, on the instroke, rock forward and up (use your feet for leverage), again staying close for maximum clitoral stimulation and bringing the glans directly into the area where the ever-elusive G spot is supposed to be.

With a little practice (I'm sure she won't mind helping), you can limit the motion to the lower body only, thus increasing your stamina by expending less energy than with the traditional in-out movement. Some other nice side effects are the increased intimacy of staying face to face mere inches apart and increased friction for you. This is definitely one for a romantic evening with someone you love.

P.S.: For those with staying problems, you needn't maintain an erection if you limit the motion a little bit. Once it's in, it can stay in all night, hard or soft! She may never notice you went limp till you're up again.

—D.W., Decatur, Illinois

221. Take Charge

How can I (or we) make foreplay more exciting for my boyfriend so that he will spend more time at it? He spends less than a minute licking my boobs, then moves into position to enter me. Needless to say, my body is seldom lubricated sufficiently for comfortable penetration. Is there something I can do to make him enjoy foreplay?

—S.D., Scarsdale, New York

You should take charge of the next few lovemaking sessions. Tell your boyfriend that you are going to make love to him the way you want him to make love to you. Give him a total body massage, tease his nipples, brush your lips along his thighs, the usual stuff. While you are doing this, position your body so that you give yourself some indirect clitoral stimulation. When you are lubricated, jump his bones from a dizzy height. When you switch back to your normal roles, make noise, pull your hair, claw his back, and so forth. You can give directions in bed without sounding like Ilse, She-Wolf of the SS. Make a set of flash cards that say: HIGHER. LOWER. HARDER. SOFTER. FASTER. SLOWER. LONGER. SHORTER. OH, MY GOD, I'M COMING. *Or simply challenge him: "Let's see how many orgasms you can give me before you enter." Anticipation is also an effective form of foreplay. Earlier in the day, why not fantasize about your boyfriend? That way, you won't have as far to go to catch up when he starts making his moves. Finally, don't think of it as foreplay, think of it as play. Put on a blindfold and play with the nonvisual senses. Ask him to make a list of fantasies or sexual positions that he has dreamed of trying. Make a list of your own. Put them in a hat and draw them out, one at a time.*

222. The Perfect Hand Job

AIDS forced us to look at lovemaking anew. How do we make sex exciting, sensual, and safe? Writers started to re-examine the basics. Peter Brooks's *Terrific Sex in Fearful Times* managed to bring an upbeat tone to the national conversation about sex. Not only did he write about such previously taboo subjects as male masturbation, he found delicious variety in the act. Here are his suggestions (which, by the way, work well when performed by your partner):

The Double Whammy

How about going double or nothing! Bring both well-lubricated hands down on his shaft. Some cocks are so big they require two hands. If your partner's doesn't, then use the other hand to caress and lightly flutter his balls, or tighten it around the base of his shaft. If both hands fit along the length of the shaft, move them together, up and down, in the typical pumping motion. Pretend you're holding a baseball bat and are about to score a grand slam. You can also vary the directions of your hands, one up, one down at the same time.

The Anvil Stroke

Bring one hand down, letting it stroke the penis from the top all the way to the bottom. When it hits the bottom, release it. Meanwhile, you're bringing your corresponding hand down to the top of the shaft, creating an alternating beating motion, hence the name Anvil Stroke. Think of those blacksmith duos who keep up a double-beat pounding motion as they beat that rod of iron on a piping-hot anvil.

The Shuttle Cock

Take the penis in both hands, fingers lightly touching the sides of the shaft. In order to visualize the position, think of yourself holding a clarinet. Now flick the penis back and forth between your two hands by holding on to the loose skin of the shaft. Shuttling it back and forth in this manner may not seem incredibly thrilling to him at first, but pretty soon, as it builds up momentum, it will drive him out of his mind.

223. Breast Sex

My wife and I have been married for five years and enjoy a good sexual relationship. She is not as adventurous in bed as I would like, but that hasn't presented any problems. One sex act I tried and enjoyed before I was married was, well, to put it bluntly, fucking women between the tits. I would like to do this with my wife as foreplay or as an alternative to more standard forms of intercourse. My problem is, I can't think of a different way to name the act. Telling her "I want to fuck you between the tits" is likely to turn her off before a discussion can start. Any ideas on better phrasing?

—B.N., Juneau, Alaska

Why do you have to ask? It's not as though you're asking your wife to have sex with your dogsled team. If you are into oral sex, have your wife lie down on the bed. Straddle her with your penis between her lips. At an opportune moment, move down so that the shaft of the penis is between her breasts. (You may be able to do both at once.) Or, one night when you are giving her a hot-oil massage, give special attention to her breasts, then use your penis as a kind of dipstick. If you have access to an adult video store, rent Lilith Unleashed. *One of the female leads actively uses her breasts to make love to her partner. In short, it's not something that you do* to *her, but* for *her or with* her. *And maybe you'll find that it's* her *fantasy.*

224. Breast Behavior

In response to the letter in the July Playboy Advisor from B.N. of Juneau, Alaska, regarding the art of making love with a lady's breasts, I would like to offer some suggestions on techniques.

While she is giving you oral loving, you can slide your penis from her lips until it is between her breasts. Then begin sliding it in and out of her cleavage, and on each upstroke, she can take your penis between her lips. It is important to encourage her to be active in sharing this pleasure. When you and your lady are making love, pay special attention to her breasts. Praise their beauty, their warmth, their softness. Caress and fondle them lovingly, worship them with your lips and your tongue until both of you are hot for each other. Her breasts should be well lubricated with saliva, vaginal secretions, or some other kind of lubricant to prevent any discomfort to either of you, as well as to make it sexier and more fun. When her breasts and your penis are all slicked up, use your penis to caress her nipples, circling your glans around her areolae, and gently press the tip of her nipple into the opening of your urethra. Gentleness is the key when doing this! It is guaranteed to drive both of you to incredible heights of passion. Caress her breasts thoroughly with your penis, and then slide it between them. Have her squeeze her breasts around your penis while you begin thrusting back and forth slowly, gradually increasing the tempo. Play with her nipples while you are thrusting, and you can also reach behind you to caress her clitoris and vaginal lips to add to her pleasure. As your excitement mounts toward orgasm, you may want to slow down or even stop your breast-humping to make it last longer, or you may want to increase your tempo and really go for it. When you reach your peak, let it go all over her breasts, nipples, lips, face, and hair. Your lady will be so hot that she may have an orgasm at the same time you do. Gently and lovingly massage all of your semen into her breasts and nipples with your penis after both of you have finished. I guarantee that both you and your lady will enjoy this beautiful form of lovemaking. I hope my suggestions will help others enjoy tit-loving as much as I enjoy it.

—J.B., Baltimore, Maryland

225. The Erotic Tool Kit

I read your request for portable sex toy kits with some amusement. Have you ever tried to take a gym bag filled with handcuffs and vibrators and furry mittens through airport security? And you don't want to lose something to some cranky baggage handler. I've found that a few leather thongs do the trick quite nicely. A girlfriend in college introduced me to them— we used to dance each of us holding one cord so that it touched the other's body. I would draw it across her breasts, loop it around her waist to draw her closer, tie it around her thigh like a garter. You can grip a short length and flick it back and forth across a nipple. She would draw the thong between her labia. She would fold a thong and use it like a riding crop to set a rhythm, or combine light flicks with kisses. We used the thong instead of handcuffs. (Have you ever tied a woman's big toes together? Or just her thumbs?) And, of course, there were the more obvious bondage and light whipping games.

—N.B., Hartford, Connecticut

Not to mention, if your luggage breaks, you can tie it closed.

226. The Foot Job

During lovemaking, my husband will start licking my feet and sucking on my toes one by one. It also drives him crazy whenever I am barefoot, wearing sandals, open-toed pumps, high-heeled open-toed dress shoes, fishnet stockings, or see-through hose. I have always had a desire to masturbate my husband with my feet, instead of always using my hands and fingers to get him off. About the closest I have come to that is that when we are in a restaurant, I will sometimes slide off my shoes under the table and place one or both of my feet in his lap and gently caress his crotch by running one or both of my big toes up and down his zipper, which usually produces an erection. He will tell me to stop for fear of exploding in his pants.

Is there such a thing as foot sex? Can a woman give a man a foot or toe job? If so, how is it supposed to be done? Is there a right or wrong technique?

—D.H., Flint, Michigan

You're on the right track. Next time you're in a restaurant, play toe football—for keeps. After he explodes in his pants (actually, we think he'll merely erupt, not explode), spill a glass of water in his lap and make sounds of dismay to cover his cries of orgasm. You can also try this at home, reclining on opposite ends of a couch, maybe during 60 Minutes. *Or try it during your bridge game.*

227. If I Had a Hammer

My wife is a totally different lover during anal sex. She came a gasping, breathless long one that left her voice low and hoarse till she got her wind back, and she clutched and grasped at me with her heels and hands to drive me home. The usual bedroom posture is a bit trying—for instance, kneeling on a water bed, trying to retain your balance while you lean forward on a woman's back to fondle her breasts, kiss her neck, and reach her clitoris. I don't like water beds anyway, so I built my slat bed to be just the right height to allow a woman to bend over the edge and have everything within reach while I stand on an even keel. This keeps me from hurrying or losing my balance, which is not a good thing, as the anus is more tender than the vagina.

I have also made a stool out of a toilet seat that will stand athwart my middle when I am recumbent on the floor. It's a big, comfortable one. A woman can get on this, draw up her feet, and hug her knees, leaving her clitoris and labia exposed to finger gently like a key pad. You can very agreeably while away a whole Sunday afternoon this way, rocking to and fro to orgasm after orgasm. I have put an upholstered back on the thing so she can relax occasionally. It works a treat! When not in use, it stands in a corner of my living room with a potted plant growing up through the middle. The seat is one of those horseshoe affairs, open at the front, and with a pillow under your head, it also facilitates cunnilingus. But it doesn't explain to me why some folks get a rise out of being fucked up the backside.

—M.P., New York, New York

228. Talk Dirty Blindfolded

I have a boyfriend who talks dirty in bed. Not with swear words or anything like that. He makes up long, involved fantasies using the names of people we know. Usually he asks me to imagine that we are having a ménage à trois with one of our female acquaintances. He will say, "And Mary is stroking your breasts, just so. Her hand is touching your clitoris, delicately." Or, "Jennifer is pressing her breasts to your back, cupping your breasts with her hands." Sometimes I wear a blindfold and pretend that it is actually happening as he describes it. Is that weird? He has never even hinted at making the fantasy a reality, so some of my initial nervousness has disappeared. I even find that his soundtrack fuels my imagination. Maybe I don't have a problem after all.

—B.J., Chicago, Illinois

229. The Human Buzz Bomb

I have been avoiding writing to you about my secret oral sex trick for a long time, but here goes. Dildos and vibrators stimulate the clitoris and drive most women wild once they get used to them. There are several problems with those artificial props: They are cold, hard, require batteries or cords, and the vibrating sensations are very limited. My secret is to gently buzz your lips on the clit for a long time and vary the speed with your breath. Once the lady gets used to the sound of you giving her raspberries on her clit, she will climax harder and longer than with any vibrator! Simply practice passing a long stream of air through your lips on your arm until you can control the buzzing or flapping. The more you practice, the easier it gets, and you will achieve more variety in the vibrations. Then start buzzing your lips on her thigh so that she can get used to the funny sound and unique sensation. It won't be long before she is ready to feel it on her clit. The result is a hot pair of lips buzzing on her clit at any speed or pressure she likes. By taking long and deep breaths between buzzing, you can continue this personal vibrator for as long as the lady likes. One word of caution before you try this: Many women find it so exciting and orgasmic that they lose their breath from screaming, so stop to let them catch their breath. A woman can also use this technique on a man by buzzing her lips on the sensitive skin behind the head of his penis. It is very exciting and very unusual. Please let me know if you have ever heard of this and what results you have found. Try it; you'll love it!

—R.M., Irvine, California

Think of the money you'll save on batteries alone.

230. Toe Jam Football

I recently met a wonderful lady. I'm twenty-three, she's twenty-nine. We were watching TV one night on her couch with her legs on my lap. She asked me to give her a foot massage to help her relax. That seemed to really turn her on quickly. She then asked me if I would start licking her feet and sucking her toes. Much to my surprise, I actually liked doing this. She started to get really hot and excited. We found ourselves on the floor, lying on our backs opposite each other, head to foot. She unzipped my pants and started to masturbate me with one foot while I was sucking and kissing her other foot. I loved it. It felt fantastic. She said no one else would do this to her. Now I'm confused. Is this normal? Do I have a foot fetish? Does she?

—G.S., Akron, Ohio

No. You just have—are you ready for this?—responsive feet. It sounds like a name for a dance band, doesn't it?

231. The Complete Erotic Tool Kit

I had to reply to your erotic tool kit inquiry. My case of accessories is about as comprehensive as possible. I met my lover six years ago. Both of us are middle-aged and married to beautiful people who nevertheless are sexually indifferent. We clicked over coffee and, in the space of one wonderful eclectic morning, decided to sample every facet of our wide and varied fantasies. Unfortunately, our intimate time together is usually not more than one afternoon a week, but, oh, what an action-packed event. The tool kit started out as an overnight shoulder bag. It has now grown into a large attaché case that seems to weigh a ton. I won't regale your readers with the complete inventory of 154 items, but let me list some of the highlights. The tool kit contains every form of transparent panty and body stocking, corset, whispies and waspies, French cutout bras, garter belts, and crotchless undies. There are wigs, gloves, patent-leather boots, a feather duster, and a cowhide whip. There are body paints; bath oils; plastic pegs with carefully stretched springs (nipples can stand only so much pain); a black mask; dildos in three sizes; and a hard-rubber vibrating butterfly, which has since been discarded in favor of the single and double vibrating eggs (the latter often slip into specially prepared pockets in a black bra or can be inserted anally and vaginally simultaneously). Then there is menthol shaving cream and lip balm for the nipples. We even have a tiny brush and comb for pubic grooming. Oh, yes, and there is my cock ring, which she makes me wear along with my wet-look bikini with the cock hole when I'm face-down on the rubber sheet. There is also petroleum jelly and massage cream, rubber panties, a dog collar and handcuffs, ben-wa balls, and anal beads. I know that when we open the kit next Wednesday, there'll be something I forgot to report. I'm always a three-timer in that many hours, and for a guy pushing sixty, you have to agree that that ain't half bad.

—W.H., Los Angeles, California

What, no condoms? We hope you tip the bellboy well.

232. The Teaching Aid

My wife has a fantasy of my giving head to another guy while she watches. She claims that by doing that, she would be able to tell what I wanted her to do to me (she figures that I would know what I was doing, I guess). Do you have any suggestions on how we can get a consenting third party? I would appreciate your thoughts and comments.

—R.A., Utica, New York

Your wife wants to know what you like? Put her fingers into your mouth. Pretend they are a penis. Do unto her as you would have her do onto you. You can practice cunnilingus the same way. Fold your thumb against your hand so that it resembles labia. Let her attack, et cetera. You can do this in public.

233. Multiple Male Orgasm

Sometimes, if I take the time to work myself up when masturbating, I am able to ejaculate modest amounts of semen without fully climaxing. I am not referring to the small drops of what is commonly called pre-come fluid. On occasion, I am able to do this once or twice before the final crash, during one masturbatory session. The feeling during the entire episode with proper control can be a pleasant one from just skirting the outer edges of orgasm. Sometimes I am almost convinced that this is similar to the multiple orgasms that some women experience. Is this common among men?

—Y.H., Cedar Rapids, Iowa

Some men can separate the emission of semen from the contractions that normally accompany orgasm. The result is something that mimics the female multiple orgasm but is different on several counts. Men who indulge in this practice report that the final orgasm (with all the fireworks) is the best. Afterward, they lose their erection. Women who experience multiple orgasms do not reach a final orgasm per se. They move from plateau to orgasm to plateau to orgasm like a stone skipping across the water. Amen.

234. Condom Carrier

Where does one carry a condom so that he's prepared in case a too-good-to-pass-up opportunity presents itself? A wallet seems to be a poor storage place. So

does a pocket in a pair of trousers. I've been pleasantly surprised often enough on first dates that I'd like to have condoms available, without their being conspicuous in case nothing happens. Any suggestions?
—J.S., Hoffman Estates, Illinois

We have seen school ties with little pockets on the back for condoms, Jockey shorts with a little watch pocket for a condom, and customized jewelry (condom earrings, condom watch fobs). Usually these are sold as novelty items at sex shops. If you are looking for a tasteful carrying case, why not convert a cigarette case or old pocket watch? We know someone who carries condoms in the leather sheath where he used to carry his Buck knife, though it does tend to destroy the line of his tux. The obvious solution is to take your date back to your place for a nightcap. Or be gentlemanly enough to suggest safer forms of sex—a few hours of oral sex, touching each other, or playing spin the vibrator. Not having a condom doesn't rule out sex, just intercourse.

235. The Mile-High Club

A friend and I were talking about the Mile-High Club. She wants to make love to her boyfriend in his private plane. I said that I didn't think private planes counted toward membership in the club. What do you say? Is membership in the Mile-High Club earned from any intimate episode in any aircraft, or just in commercial airliners? Also, what sexual acts grant membership? I maintain that it's only intercourse that counts. If you manage to get into some heavy petting or oral sex, does that count toward membership or just give you membership in the half-Mile-High Club?

—S.J., Chicago, Illinois

What do you think this is? The Internet? This is the kind of topic that chat groups obsess over endlessly. It strikes us that the people who have sex on private airplanes don't need to belong to a club. As for what constitutes mile-high sex, certain things seem obvious. You probably don't earn advantage miles by making an obscene phone call to a friend from an in-flight telephone (although try that the next time you fly). You probably don't gain membership by obtaining an orgasm solo (I'm just exercising my laptop). Beyond that, it seems pointless to distinguish between orgasms. Certainly the couple who achieve fully nude simultaneous orgasm from 69 in the overhead compartment is as entitled to applause as the couple who sneak into the restroom on a red-eye for a little vertical play. We personally think that anything that goes on under those blankets is worth the effort.

236. Now, Kids, Don't Try This at Camp

I sometimes enjoy doing odd things during sex. For example, two years ago, in upstate New York, my girlfriend and I had intercourse while we were water skiing. I held on to the tow rope while she wrapped her legs around my waist. (With a little practice, we learned that it helped to be well on our way toward orgasm before signaling my friend in the boat to pull us up.)

Doing it in odd situations is so much more exciting. Is this feeling common, or do I have a fetish?

—C.A.B., New York, New York

Our question: Were you wearing a condom at the time? Practice safe sex at all times, even when on the end of a tow rope. You don't have a fetish, just two good friends. For those of you who want to try an aquatic rush, consider renting a personal watercraft, one of those sit-down models. Rearrange your bathing suits, find a comfortable position for penetration, and let the throttle and steering do the rest.

237. What Would You Say If We Played Out of Tune?

Have you ever heard of an anal violin? I came across the phrase in a story about China but could not figure out what the device was—except that it had something to do with sex. Any clues?

—W.O., New Orleans, Louisiana

Sex A to Z by Robert Goldman and Kenneth N. Andersen defines the anal violin as follows: "An anal masturbation device of the Orient consisting of a hard-boiled egg or a wooden or ivory ball to which a catgut string is attached. The egg or ball is inserted in the anus, the string is made taut and a partner uses a violin bow to make it vibrate. The device was especially popular among the eunuchs of the Ottoman Empire." Makes for a wonderful image, doesn't it? A bunch of eunuchs sitting around making chamber music. Our guess is that the anal violin was the only stringed in-

strument not featured on A Prairie Home Companion.
Thank heaven for batteries.

238. Nipple Redux

My girlfriend says that she can reach orgasm from
nipple stimulation alone. Since I never engage in nipple
stimulation alone, I haven't witnessed the phenomenon
firsthand. Have you ever heard of such a thing?

—S.D., Chicago, Illinois

*Kids today. Whatever happened to heavy petting? It
sounds to us as though your girlfriend has given you a challenge, and a subtle hint that you are rushing foreplay. Give
her breasts an hour or so of your undivided attention and
see what happens. Or take along a feather duster and tal-
cum powder. Consider drawing a string of pearls across her
skin. Try finger-painting or drawing an elaborate tattoo with
a felt-tip pen. Everything you need to know about foreplay
you learned in kindergarten.*

239. Squeaky Clean

The Thai body scrub is the ultimate in personal hygiene. You perform it in a shower, at the bottom of an
empty pool, or in a basement—wherever there is a floor
drain. Inflate a small air mattress. You lie on the mattress.
Your girlfriend rubs your body with bath oil, then rubs

her own body with bath oil, then dumps a bucket of soap-suds over the mattress. She scrubs your body with her body. It's called slipping and sliding. The inevitable happens. Then hose everything down and wait until next washday.

240. The Sundial

I recently met a man who is into obscure Oriental sex techniques. He says that a Taoist master once suggested harnessing the energy of the sun for sex by walking into a garden with an erection and pointing at the sun. You're supposed to imagine the power coming into the organ and then, when you finally make love, radiating into your partner. Is this guy pulling my leg?
—D.W., San Francisco, California

Pardon me while I radiate on your face? Something like this is mentioned in The Taoist Secrets of Love *by Master Mantak Chia. It takes all kinds to fill the freeways. The technique is a great way to tell time in the absence of a wristwatch. The only benefit to sex that we see is when you ask your partner to apply the sun block.*

[Editor's note: We have reconsidered all those Oriental exercises that ask you to imagine sexual forces moving through your body. A metaphor is as good as a massage. We doubt that there is free-roaming energy, other than what we call attention. Sex isn't what happens, it's what you notice. And we've had lovers persuade us that sex is solar-powered: Lying on a nude beach, let the sun lick your body. See what gets warm first.]

241. Fantasex

I've been dating a girl who approaches sex like improv night at some repertory company. She likes to play make-believe games in bed, assuming different roles. One night we'll be a professor and student, another night a hired killer and a witness held hostage, or maybe a porn director and an aspiring actress. She gets into this, but I'm a little lost. What's going on? Any suggestions?

—T.W., Seattle, Washington

Maybe she got hold of a copy of Rolf Milonas's Fantasex, *which contains a collection of roles and sexual plays for couples to perform. The man has a choice of characters ranging from TV anchorman, Arab sheik, Nazi officer, blind genius, delivery boy, and hunted guerrilla leader to gynecologist; the woman may choose from roles such as branch librarian, drill sergeant, high school cheerleader, senator, prison matron, wanted terrorist, and suburban housewife. Depending on the mood, you and your lover can choose roles, or just one of you can pick the role. Then you get to pick a play: Milonas has scenarios such as two people dancing together or the woman kneeling on a chair while the man enters her from behind. We guess the thrill comes from trying to imagine how an Arab sheik would enter a branch librarian. Ask yourself what quality your girlfriend is getting at in her choice of characters—is it submissiveness, assertiveness, tenderness, roughness, drama? Fantasy games can be profoundly silly or incredibly liberating—it depends on the power of your imaginations and your willingness to suspend disbelief. Some couples have a hard time becoming sexual—they need a transition time to shift from the con-*

cerns of everyday life to the soft fascination of the bedroom. Some do it with a favorite piece of music, some with a glass of wine before the fire. Why not a parlor game?

242. The Ladder to Heaven

Here's a great sexual technique to share with your readers. My girlfriend and I were painting our apartment not long ago. I was getting off on watching her climb up and down the stepladder, and finally when the painting was done, I interrupted her descent by tearing off her panties and performing cunnilingus on her while she was on the ladder. When we moved into round two, she simply turned around and arched her back against the ladder, holding on to the rung above her head. It was incredible. Have you ever heard of sex on a ladder?

—D.F., Atlanta, Georgia

How many southerners does it take to change a light-bulb? Never mind. Once you start thinking about it, ladders are everywhere. You can sneak into a playground after dark and use the ladder on the slide. You can haunt the stacks at the public library and send your girlfriend to find obscure texts located on the top shelf. (Maybe this is how the Arab sheik enters the branch librarian?) You can leave a ladder in the corner of a loft apartment without having to explain it the way you would a rack or a ceiling mirror.

243. An Oldie but Goody

My latest boyfriend has a strange taste in lovemaking. After he enters me, he insists that I bring myself to orgasm by touching myself. Then, after the contractions cease, he wants me to continue clenching those muscles until he reaches orgasm. It's a bit of a workout, but he says he loves the feel of my inner muscles, that a woman's cunt is not a passive organ. Have you ever heard of this?

—M.C., Santa Fe, New Mexico

It's called pompoir. Alex Comfort mentions it no less than five times in The Joy of Sex. *He traced the practice to Sir Richard Burton, who once gave this advice: "She must close and constrict the yoni until it holds the lingam as with a finger, opening and shutting at her pleasure, and finally acting as the hand of the Gopala girl who milks the cow. This can be learned only by long practice and especially by throwing the will into the part affected."*

Comfort called it pompoir, but Americans with a taste for the technical just call the movement Kegels. A great way to have sex undetected on creaky old beds in your parents' house.

244. The Clitoris as Penis

I became curious about my body and soon learned that touching my clitoris caused it to quiver and grow stiff, which really felt good. By the time I was eighteen I could caress my clitoris until it stiffened and lengthened to about an inch and protruded from the lips of my vagina. I finally lost my virginity to a sophomore who was exceptionally considerate of me, but who was also amazed at how large my clitoris became when I was sexually aroused. We experimented by rubbing my clitoris against the opening of his erect penis to produce pleasurable sensation unlike anything else imaginable.

—B.G., Minneapolis, Minnesota

245. Sexy Sangria

Easily the most eye-catching title on my bookshelf is something called *Oral Sex Made Easy*, published by the International Sex Institute in 1982. The anonymous author was an oral sex sommelier, giving this advice:

One of the special benefits of oral-genital sex is that it can titillate the taste buds as well as the genitals. Many individuals lovingly pour sweet wine, champagne or some other liquid on their lover's chest, abdomen or pubic region, then sensually lick it off as it runs in rivulets to and over the genital region. Sweet wines are perhaps the most popular. Champagne, the modern beverage of romance, adds the sensation of effervescence to the one receiving the libation, but its dry flavor does not combine well with the natural aroma of the woman's vulva. A bubbly sweet wine might be a better choice. Tastes vary, but it is advisable not to apply to the genital region any alcoholic beverage stronger than wine with 12 percent to 14 percent alcohol. Though some people are excited by the burning sensation caused by stronger liquors, most find it merely painful. Orange juice is a popular enhancement of oral sex. It offers the benefit of neutralizing vulva odors to those individuals who for some reason are not fond of the genital scent. If orange juice is used, it should be squeezed a drop at a time from a fresh orange onto the genital region. Other liquids or semi-liquids popular with devotees of oral genital sex include honey, melted ice cream and whipped cream. These offer the advantage of viscosity, enabling them to be dripped onto the man's penis as well as on the woman's vulva. For hygiene's sake it's imperative that genital regions bathed in such substances be licked clean by the oral partner or that the genital partner follow the lovemaking with a cleansing of the genitals. . . . Some individuals enjoy placing small pieces of fruit in the woman's vagina, then removing them with tongue, lips or teeth. Strawberries, slices of banana, seedless orange sections, pieces of melons and slices of apples work well, as do most other fruits that can be sliced into small sections. Obviously, it is necessary to clean such fruit well before sexplay.

246. Palm Funday

My wife and I recently made a discovery that I find truly fascinating. We have found that by placing the palm of my hand on her lower abdomen—just above the pubic area—and massaging gently, she can achieve orgasm after orgasm. She tells me the sensation is from the pressure on her uterus and ovaries and that it wasn't until after she had a baby a couple of years ago that this area became so sensitive. Having been brought up on the Masters and Johnson idea that most female orgasms are clitoral in nature, I am intrigued by this new discovery. How unique is the technique?

—K.B., New Haven, Connecticut

A lot of people misinterpret Masters and Johnson's finding about clitoral sensitivity to mean that only direct stimulation produces orgasm, or that it is the only route to orgasm. Many women cannot tolerate direct stimulation and prefer indirect methods such as the one you have discovered. (Also, childbirth changes the genital anatomy, in some cases increasing blood flow to the erect clitoris, thus making it easier to climax.)

247. Grease

I'd like to share a type of lovemaking I discovered while giving my girlfriend a back rub. She was lying on her stomach and I was kneeling astride her just behind her rear end. We were both nude. I found that by leaning forward, my growing penis would find a happy home nestled between her lovely ass cheeks, toward the top of her buttocks. I was massaging her using a skin cream for a lubricant. Without a moment's hesitation, I lubed my penis and my girlfriend's rear end as well. Thrusting between the top of her cheeks felt great on the underside of my penis, but it didn't seem like enough stimulation to bring me to orgasm. So with a little more lubrication, I simply placed my right hand on top of my penis, pressing it snugly against my lover.

Now I was thrusting my penis from my wrist to my fingertips, while still massaging my girlfriend with my free hand. This soon brought me to a wonderful climax. She loved the whole experience. (She complains of soreness sometimes after intercourse. This way there was no penetration, no soreness, no risk of pregnancy.)
—R.T., Boston, Massachusetts

Take what you've learned from this and turn your girlfriend over. A front rub, plus a little lubrication, may take care of the soreness.

248. Public Sex: The Downside

My husband and I have a serious problem. I have always loved to have sex in our car while parked in a crowded parking lot at the shopping mall. Recently we were caught by a store clerk and reported to the police. There were no charges filed, so I figured everything was okay. But it seems that after my husband had that talk with the policeman, he thinks we shouldn't make love in the parking lot anymore because it's too kinky. I have told him that I can't reach orgasm unless we make love as we always have, in the parking lot. He has suggested vibrators and X-rated movies, but it just isn't the same. Can you convince him that this practice is not that kinky? I really don't think it is, do you?
—C.J., Charleston, South Carolina

Actually, we do think it's a little kinky. That's why it's so much fun. [For married folks, parking on lover's lane, or in the garage, is a good way to have sex before the hassle of taking the babysitter home. For students with roommates or parents, it may be the only form of sex.] Why not examine the situation and find out what it is that appeals to you? Is it the car that makes you carnal? Then have sex on deserted highways. Is it the thrill of potential discovery? (Your husband has found that actual discovery may not be so thrilling.) Try renting a hotel room and leaving the window shades open. Make love in a three-pictures-for-a-dollar photo booth and let some passerby stumble upon the pictures. Wear masks. The worst thing you can do is wield your orgasm like a nonnegotiable demand. There are plenty of ways to add a touch of excitement to sex—it's up to you to find them.

249. Attitude Is Everything

I deeply love my wife, but I think our sex life has become boring. Can you suggest any thought-provoking books?

—K.W., Portland, Oregon

Carol G. Wells, author of Right Brain Sex: Using Creative Visualization to Enhance Sexual Pleasure, *suggests this little test. For each of the following situations, rate yourself for predictability, giving yourself a five if you're very predictable and a one if you're never predictable:*

1. *The time of day we have sex*
2. *The day of the week we have sex*
3. *The place we have sex*
4. *Who initiates*
5. *How we get started*
6. *What we are wearing*

7. What we do to arouse each other
8. The order of events
9. What we say or don't say during sex
10. What we do after we finish sex

If your score is thirty or above, you deserve to be bored. More than anything, if you want to change your sex life, you have to change your attitude toward sex. Wells provides a target, something she calls the sexually lustful couple, partners who

intentionally stay in bed on a weekday or weekend morning and enjoy each other's company; watch less television in favor of a romp in the sack; let the laundry and lawn wait instead of their lust; are playful and uninhibited about their sexual desires; feel little rejection when one or the other is not in the mood, because they know it won't be weeks or months before there is another opportunity; value sex too much to use it as a battleground for other areas of disagreement; recognize the need for transitions and so go out of their way to set a sexy, romantic mood with music, candles, oils or special dinners; tease each other with innuendoes to keep lust alive; are more experimental and willing to try new behaviors, are more likely to masturbate in front of their partner; enjoy sharing sexual fantasies and erotic talk; are more flexible in their conditions for sex—i.e. time of day, place, rules of cleanliness, etc.; communicate their sexual preferences to each other; are not ashamed to let their children know they have sexual needs; go into the bedroom, shut the door and tell the children they want private time.

250. The Tit and the Frenulum

My boyfriend and I were reading a sex manual the other night and came across some interesting information. According to the author, the frenulum— the little flap of skin where the glans and the foreskin meet—is the most sensitive part of the penis. My boyfriend's reaction was, "big deal." It is not something that really comes into play during intercourse. I've tried flicking it with my tongue during oral sex, with some effect. Can you check your files for any other techniques that involve this sensitive area?

—L.R., Dallas, Texas

Kneel in front of your lover and brush your nipples across the tip of his penis.

251. Think of a Bic Lighter

We read your letter about the frenulum being the most sensitive part of the penis and would like to add our two cents: my girlfriend treats my erection like a Bic lighter. She flicks her thumb across the frenulum, or for variety, rubs in tiny circular motions on the loose skin. I'm not sure that the area is more sensitive—it just provides some variety in touch and sensation. Also, during oral sex and intercourse, a simple up-and-down thrusting motion seems to miss the frenulum. We have found that if my girlfriend puts her lips just over the crown of the penis and does a twisting motion, she creates a wonderful sensation, a kind of ring of fire.

—D.K., Boston, Massachusetts

252. Avoid the Clitoris?

I've had women complain that I spend too much time on clitoral stimulation, or that I move to the genitals too quickly. One woman went so far as to say that all the articles in women's magazines heralding a return to romance are really a call to go back to whole-body sensuousness—i.e., everything except the clitoris. I'm open to suggestions. Are there any erogenous zones worth investigating?

—W.I., Memphis, Tennessee

Prior to Masters and Johnson, everyone used to say that the clitoris was a monument in Greece. Then we learned that it was the sexual nerve center for women and paid it a lot, perhaps too much attention. At college lectures we used to tell women that the single most important thing they could teach their boyfriends was the location of the clitoris. "You'll appreciate it, and the next girl he goes out with will appreciate it." Still true, but there is a backlash. Remember the Monty Python movie in which John Cleese warned schoolboys, "You don't go leaping for the clitoris like a bull at the gate." There are a host of other hot spots. The entire body is an erogenous zone. Every now and then one area gets trendy—first the clitoris, then the G spot, then the Y spot (you touch it and your girlfriend asks, "Why are you doing that?"). Eventually even the most sensitive area gets overrun with tourists. We've seen books proclaiming that the meaning of life can be found in the nape of the neck, the navel, the boy knobs of the pelvis, the juncture of thigh and torso, the back of the knee, the buttocks, the spine, and the small of the back. One of the most intriguing suggestions is to treat body hair as an erogenous zone. Try running your fingernails across the downlike hairs on your lover's back and you'll see what we mean.

253. Bobbing for Apples

One of my fraternity brothers says that he attended a party where the revelers played a sexual version of bobbing for apples. They would take a couple and tie their hands behind their backs and watch while they tried to make out. Sounds like bullshit to me. What do you think?

—E.M., Houston, Texas

They should try it naked. This has been a party game since the nineteenth century (probably because you need a third person to tie the second person's hands). It has been the source of sexual tension in every Hollywood hostage/getaway scene ever made. You can try this in private, simply asking your partner to hold her hands behind her back while performing oral sex.

254. Slam Dance

My girlfriend gets turned on by something I think is a bit strange, though highly erotic. Here is her favorite way to have sex: We lie on a soft blanket on a carpeted floor. She lies flat on it, face-down. I lie down on her back and penetrate her vagina from the rear. As I pound her pelvis and pubic bone into the floor, the shock waves vibrate through her pubic bone and stimulate her clitoris, etc. She can come over and over until exhausted. I've asked her just what is going on inside her when we do this. She said that she was not sure but that she used to masturbate when she was younger by lying on the floor in the same position and rubbing and gently hitting her pubic bone on the carpet. Have you ever heard of such a thing?

—J.H., Elgin, Illinois

Did you once live in the apartment above ours?

255. Pillow Talk

I finally took some advice you had given in past columns and asked my girlfriend to show me how she masturbated. She introduced me to her old friend—a pillow that she squeezed between her legs. She would rock against it, stimulating herself until she reached orgasm. I was aroused and asked for a repeat. She rolled over and I entered her doggie-style. She kept the pillow beneath her and rubbed her clitoris against the satin cover while I thrust from behind. The effect was explosive. I just wondered if you had ever heard of a ménage à trois with a pillow?

—C.Y., Hartford, Connecticut

Group sex with laundry? Yes, we've heard of this. You can also utilize armchairs and sofas for a third leg.

256. The Imaginary Ménage

Watching an X-rated movie the other night, my girlfriend commented on how hot one particular scene was. A woman was stretched out on a bed, half on/half off, performing fellatio on her partner. While her lips and hands encircled the man's erection, her hips were thrusting against the edge of the bed, rubbing her clitoris along the sheet. We tried the same maneuver and it was astonishing. My girlfriend confessed that she felt like she was having sex with two men at once. We've since played with other positions that bring in ghost lovers—say, I enter her from behind and touch her clitoris with one hand, while offering her my fingers to suck on. She treats my free hand exactly as she would an erection.

—J.L., San Francisco, California

257. Cheers

Under sex tricks learned from porn movies, include this: making love on a bar stool. In a John Leslie movie, a male actor in a restaurant/bar enters a woman sitting on a bar stool. (She is wearing leather or latex chaps, with no bottom, to facilitate sex, but you can do the same thing by lifting your partner's dress in a dark bar, or just doing it naked in the rec room.) The height is perfect, your partner can throw her arms along the bar for support, and if you want a particularly subtle sensation, she can rotate the bar stool back and forth.

258. Wish I Didn't Know Now What I Didn't Know Then

I'm a college student enjoying my first serious sexual relationship. Having grown up in the age of AIDS, I know all about birth control and safe sex, but what I don't know much about is how to make my love affair adventurous and spontaneous. What do you suggest?
—A.T., Spokane, Washington

We love this kind of question. It brings out our sixties nostalgia for the days when living an experimental life was fraught with mistakes but no real danger. Here are some suggestions: Free your libido from the same old routine. Try doing it with no foreplay, or at least with the appearance of no foreplay. Ask her to leave her underwear at home, but don't tell her why. Find a secluded corner and show her why. Or don't. Let the suspense be the experience. Try a quickie in the car. Try the exact opposite, having foreplay in a place where there is no chance for consummation. Experiment with isolating neglected senses. Capture the sounds of your lovemaking on cassette (later—after finishing that special dinner you cooked, for instance—play it back). Give her a full-service massage (include lotions, feathers, vibrators, and any rock music with a powerful bass line). Tell her stories about sex. Engage in phone sex (this will tell you a lot about her fantasies—and yours). Do something that is extremely physical that is not sexual—run together or take up Greco-Roman wrestling. Get acquainted with one organ at a time. Start with her skin. Lightly pinch every square inch of her body, or drum it lightly with your fingertips. That should take care of one date.

259. Amateur Night

When traveling recently, my boyfriend and I thought we'd incorporate some adult pleasure into our trip. We were simply looking for an adult motel with mirrors on the ceiling, X-rated movies, and a water bed—pretty tame stuff. Across five states, it became obvious that what we wanted existed on the bad side of town, isolated among warehouses and rundown buildings. Who could feel safe there? There should be a guide to adult motels. Likewise, the high point of the trip was when we decided to have some fun by my participating in amateur night at a strip bar. We eventually found a place worth walking into. I entered the contest and we had some of the hottest sex ever later that night and for a while thereafter. I thought your readers might enjoy nominating their favorite motels and strip clubs, maybe give us a directory to match the best of America's bed and breakfasts.

—A.M., Columbia, South Carolina

Nice idea, but if they make passion pits squeaky clean, then someone might get the idea that sex is wholesome. The city fathers would never allow that. Chicago has a chain of couples suites called The Sybaris—with mirrors, water beds, indoor pools, hot tubs, and steambaths—that are booked for months in advance (a weekend night can cost as much as $495). Learn to live off the land. You can order a Mylar ceiling mirror (which can be removed in seconds) from Stamford Hygienic Corporation (Box 931, Stamford, Connecticut 06904) for under twenty dollars. If you wish strip joints were as clean as health clubs, why not reverse the equation and make health clubs as sexy as strip joints? Wear an oversize ripped T-shirt with large armholes and no bra to your next workout and check the attention you get.

260. A Thrust Is Just a Thrust

How do you vary the old in and out? Oriental sex manuals provide a virtual thesaurus of thrusts. The following list comes from the *T'ung Hsuan Tzu,* by seventeenth-century physician Li T'ung Hsuan:

1. Strike out to the left and right as a brave warrior trying to break up the enemy ranks.
2. Move up and down as a wild horse bucking through a stream.

3. Pull out and push in as a group of seagulls playing on the waves.

4. Use deep thrusts and shallow teasing strokes, alternating swiftly as a sparrow picking the leftovers of rice in a mortar.

5. Make deep and shallow strokes in steady succession as a huge stone sinking into the sea.

6. Push in slowly as a snake entering a hole to hibernate.

7. Thrust swiftly as a frightened rat rushes into a hole.

8. Poise, then strike like an eagle catching an elusive hare.

9. Rise, then plunge low like a huge sailing boat braving the gale.

261. Obsession

Often I find myself looking at what I'd consider a distractingly attractive woman and thinking about what it would be like to indulge in my sexual fantasy with her: We would both be naked, lying on a couch or a bed, and I would position myself over her and begin gently kissing her shoulder. Then I'd kiss up the side of her neck to the point just below her earlobe, moving down her jaw to her chin, then to her lower lip. I'd stroke my tongue, which has been described by some women as massive, down her throat to the point between her clavicles. I'd kiss down her chest, past the area between her breasts, then back up across her breast to the nipple, around which I'd slowly lick with the tip of my tongue. Then I'd lick back to the area between her breasts and nibble my way down her torso to her navel, continuing to where her pubic hair begins. At that point, I would gently spread open her cunt and softly blow across her clit as I moved my mouth down toward it, gently taking it between my teeth and slowly rubbing the tip of my tongue up and down it. When I released it, I would extend my tongue to its fullest width, pressing it against her clit and sliding it slowly from side to side. After doing that for ten to fifteen minutes, I would resume holding her clit between my teeth, closing my lips around it and sliding my lips and teeth up and off. I'd move to the area just below her pubic hair, licking her from side to side. When she told me to stop, I'd move back up her torso to her navel, her breasts, and her shoulders and then start the whole thing over again, if she'd let me. Some people might consider it kind of strange, but I would not want her to do anything to me afterward in return, other than simply lying beside me and cuddling. Is it strange for a guy to be turned on by something most guys don't think twice about?

—K.S., Summerville, South Carolina

Nah. What we don't understand is why you took the time to write us. The only thing that got licked was the stamp. Take your act on the road. Next time you see a distractingly beautiful woman, ask her to lunch, then dinner, then tell her what you told us.

262. The Breath of Life

Recently I read an article on tantric sex. The authors described a breathing technique that supposedly

enhanced orgasm. It goes like this: "To increase the
length and power of your orgasm, start to inhale (as
slowly as possible) about halfway into its peak. The
building up feeling of climax will continue for as long as
you can sustain the inhalation. When you begin to release
the breath, do it with as much sound as possible.
Really sing out. . . . The volume of your sound
influences the volume, the depth of your orgasm. But
you want to stay in control of the sound and not use it
up too fast; the orgasm will last as long as you continue
to vocalize it in your exhalation. With practice, both
men and women can learn to keep the orgasm going for
more than one complete breath, up to four or six,
possibly more." Have you ever heard of such a thing?
—C.B., Los Angeles, California

*Sure. Lamaze classes teach women to focus on breathing
as a means of distracting themselves from the pain of childbirth. And we've heard of women who use the same techniques to focus and extend orgasm. The sexual release rides
piggyback on the physical sensations of breathing, moving the orgasm into a more total body experience. Since
orgasm—on one level, at least—is the release of tension,
anything that builds tension may increase the excitement
level. Holding your breath is one way of building tension;
so is taking a deeper breath. As for vocalizing your orgasm,
we've known people who vocalize theirs for weeks at a
time. ("Please, baby, please, baby, that was great, can we
do it again, please, baby?!?!") But let's move beyond tantric:
think high-tech. Therapists have often counseled women
who have trouble reaching orgasm to vocalize: acting out a
loud, screaming orgasm can sometimes precipitate a loud,
screaming orgasm. So why not amplify your orgasm? Suspend a microphone over your bed and run it through your*

sound system. Crank it up: You'll be inside the biggest orgasm you ever heard.

263. I Need a Miracle Every Day

My wife and I have been married almost ten years and during that time we have made love in front of a roaring fire, in the back of a van, on a picnic table, in the living room, and in the bathroom, to name a few locations. One of the most erotic experiences I have had with her involved sex in front of a roaring fire. Late one evening my wife appeared in our basement wearing nothing but a see-through camisole and a pair of crotchless panties. Needless to say, in a matter of seconds I had removed my clothes and let my rock-hard manhood spring free. After I hurriedly spread a quilt and a few pillows on the floor, we fell into each other's arms and began to fondle each other like there was no tomorrow. After several minutes of this, during which I sucked and squeezed her breasts until her nipples were hard as rocks, I moved down to where I could lick and suck her pussy and send her into sweet ecstasy. Not wanting to climax yet, we slowed down for a couple of minutes and changed positions again, moving so that she could straddle me and do deep knee bends with my dick sliding in and out of her pussy. Then she moved to her belly and raised her ass into the air, signaling that she wanted me to enter her from behind. From this position we moved to the traditional missionary. After about ten more minutes of mutual groin-grinding we both came like an earthquake. What a night! My question is, how can I persuade her to do this more often? I am easily aroused and could make love every day with this lovely lady, yet her drive is not quite as high. She is content with two or three times a week. What can I do?

—B.B., Nashville, Tennessee

Your rock-hard manhood? Mutual groin-grinding? Two or three times a week and you're complaining? Okay, here's our advice: Create an anniversary ritual. Instead of celebrating the day you got married, celebrate the days you had peak sexual experiences. Tell your wife that you would like to declare the third weekend in October Van Day and reenact that hot encounter with your gearshift of love. Declare the first day of December Fireplace Day (only next time you wear the camisole?). If you get enough of these erotic holidays going, you'll fill up a whole calendar with excuses to have great sex. One word of caution: Almost no sexual event can be duplicated. Use the anniversaries to tell each other what you did—that should get you hot and bothered—while doing something new.

264. Has Don King Heard About This?

I get off boxing with women. Over the years I've had several partners who also got off on this thrill. We would put on the gloves, work up a sweat, then fuck our brains out. Then I met a girl who did not like to box. She tried on the gloves and came up with her own scenario. She is into having sex while both of us are clad only in leather boxing gloves. Or she will strip down to high heels, boots or garters, and lipstick-red gloves. She is absolutely ravishing. She does all the punching. Even one-sided, it still works. Have I created a sexual monster? It has gotten to where she won't climb into bed without the gloves.

—J.R., Grand Rapids, Michigan

Yes, this is one of the strangest forms of foreplay we've encountered. It beats juggling with machetes, but not by much. But we also understand the power of this scenario. Anyone who has worked out with gloves knows that boxing requires the whole body: There is something about aggression that energizes every cell immediately. It flips the flight-or-fight switch. Most women equate sex with gentleness, so it's a huge turn-on to approach sex from a position of strength. Neither your body nor your ego seem fragile. You might try other whole-body approaches: wrestling, mock rape, ballet, tug of war, Indian wrestling, or isometrics.

265. Hickey High

My former girlfriend used to go nuts when I bit her neck or kissed with a lot of suction during sex. Actually, I could pinch or bite any part of her anatomy—she would draw me to her whenever she reached a certain state of excitement and I would graze. The problem? I tried this on my new girlfriend and she'd have no part of it. One of my nibbles left a hickey and she treated me as if I were some kind of sadist. Is this S/M?

—M.J., Tulsa, Oklahoma

A hickey's a sign of S/M? Maybe that's why high schools are frequently mistaken for leather bars. We happen to think that love bites are the accent marks in the language of lust. Suction equals passion. Isn't that one of Newton's laws? But not everyone agrees. One study found that 44 percent of men and 41 percent of women found the exchange of teeth marks (gentle biting) arousing. The rest seem to side with your girlfriend.

266. Boxing the Compass

There is a scene in a Walter Matthau movie in which he spends the day in bed with a woman, boxing the compass. He tries to find a sexual position for each axis of the bed. The notion applies to other pieces of furniture as well. The next time you enter a new setting with a lover, try to imagine a sexual use for every item in view. Make a pact not to leave until you've done it in the shower, on the dressing table, in the chair, on the coffee table, hanging from the chandelier, on the stairs, in the closet, in the foyer. You don't have to have an orgasm in each position or place, just some form of sexual contact. You can do this to tired old settings to revitalize your sex life. When you're done, everything you see will remind you of sex. That will lead to even more sex.

If this list seems too much, start with one piece of furniture. Take the chair in a hotel room. Your partner can sit in the chair touching herself while you watch from across the room. She can drape her legs over the arms to facilitate oral sex (you sit on the floor). You can kneel and enter her, or she can turn around for you to enter from behind. If it's a recliner, you can lower the top to bring her head to a level suited for relaxed fellatio.

You can sit in the chair, and she can put her legs over the arms and ride you with just genitals touching.

267. The Fish Bowl

Buy a large glass fish bowl. Have your lover write out ten or twenty sexual scenarios. Write some yourself. You can describe scenes from X-rated flicks, from soap operas, from fiction, from your own past with other lovers. Toss them into the bowl. Then play lotto with your love life—pulling out a scene and acting it out.

268. Interoffice Sex

Several years ago, while out of town on business, I became involved with a man who turned me on to a level higher than I could ever remember experiencing. We forced ourselves to limit our intense sexual encounter to everything except intercourse. Somehow this has eliminated the guilt of straying from our respective spouses. Time has passed and our physical distance has turned the affair into one conducted over the phone and through the mail. Part of the excitement is the fact that it is illicit. We haven't seen each other in two years, but that hasn't stopped our communication. When we can schedule the time, we have the most outrageous phone sex in our offices. Through erotic words and our hands, we are able to take each other to incredible orgasmic states. At the end of several of these phone calls, I've wound up partially dressed on my office floor with the speakerphone on. Unfortunately, sometimes we get just a few minutes of verbal turn-on, only to have to hang up due to normal workday interruptions. We both know that should we ever see each other again, our passion will supersede our sense of guilt and we'll fuck like crazy. I'm wondering if after all of this fantasy buildup, the relationship will change once we do get together. Perhaps with the mystery gone, the excitement will diminish. Based on the chemistry that connected us before (oral sex for both of us was incredible), we're sure we won't be disappointed.

—D.W., Foster City, California

Have you tried phoning home? Take what you've learned from this affair and apply it to your primary relationship. Family is the enemy of great sex: Spouses struggle to find moments of privacy into which they pour every ounce of passion. Then it's back to real life.

269. On Your Mark

My girlfriend claims that we never have enough time for sex. She likes long, lazy sessions and feels cheated by anything less. Indeed, she now fails to reach orgasm without a full production. I feel under pressure to set aside huge chunks of time when I could be off playing golf. Is there a solution?

—M.K., Casper, Wyoming

Sex, like work, expands to fill the time allotted. Your girlfriend may have set up a self-fulfilling prophecy (or is that self-defeating?). If she thinks she needs three hours, then that will become the standard. Show her that sex can be just as exciting in small bursts. Sometime soon, ask her to time herself—to see how quickly she can reach orgasm. A sprint can get your heart racing just as effectively as a marathon. When she gets it down to less than two minutes, you can start doing it in closets at parties, in telephone booths at the airport, in hotels after you've called room service, or between the time you hear the buzzer and your guest climbs three flights to your apartment. Then when she has learned to come in a few minutes, see how many orgasms you can fit into three hours or how long you can make one session last. As good as golf gets, it will never be better than sex.

270. On Timing

One of the most hilarious scenes in sexual literature occurs in the novel *Nine ½ Weeks*. The hero hangs the woman from manacles on the wall of his apartment, then sits down to watch *60 Minutes*. She cannot see what's on the television set. She just hears the periodic ticking of the signature stopwatch.

A sense of time is one of the elements of great sex. Have you considered bringing an egg timer into the bedroom?

Several sex therapists—starting with Lonnie Barbach—have discovered that women can mold their sexual response to a narrative. Women who were unable to reach orgasm after hours of stimulation found that they could climax while reading short pieces of erotic fiction. Now therapists suggest training arousal by masturbating to the same story over and over, trying to make yourself reach orgasm at the same time the fictional characters do. This also works with X-rated video—but rather than trying to reach orgasm when the director says come, try finding something earlier that arouses you. Maybe it's the curve of a neck, or the arch of a back, or the removal of a garment. Play with overreaction (maximum arousal) and no reaction (letting a movie simmer).

Make love to a favorite piece of music. Sometimes sex needs all the outside help it can get.

271. Q-Tips?

My girlfriend and I like to experiment with sex aids. I have brought her to orgasm by touching her clitoris with ice cubes, candles (unlit), feathers, paintbrushes, slices of fruit (which I subsequently consume), and most recently, Q-Tips moistened with oil or hand lotion. I've run a silk scarf lightly between her legs. A string of beads works just as well. Have I left anything out?

—W.A., Portland, Oregon

Yes. The rest of her body. Try a full-body massage with hot oil. When she is fully relaxed, touch her clitoris with your penis. You'll be surprised at the sensation. We think it's called sex.

272. Lawn Tools?

A friend and I recently were discussing the worldly topic of women, which led to a debate on who had the most innovative idea for a romantic evening. My friend won. What he had done involved the elements of excitement, suspense, and surprise. He picked up his girlfriend without previously discussing what they were going to do that night. Next he blindfolded her and said he was going to do something new. He drove back to his house and parked the car in the garage, asked her to wait a minute, got out of the car, and placed a television set and a VCR (which had been set up earlier) on the hood. They watched a romantic movie and made out like bandits. I want to take this one step further. Instead of parking in a garage, I'd go to a favorite secluded place. But to do this, I'd need either battery-operated equipment or some sort of device that a TV and VCR can plug into. Preferably, I'd like a device that can work off my car battery. Is there such a device or even a better way to watch a movie in a car?

—R.W.K., Washington, D.C.

Yes, it's called a drive-in movie. We think you need to go back to the drawing board. (We assume that you've ruled out doing Gone With the Wind *with hand puppets.) Check out the weekend rates for hotels in D.C. Rent a room, stock it with champagne, fruit, presents (a nightgown or lingerie), and, if you really are a videophile, your own VCR. Another idea: Hire a limousine to drive you to your secluded spot. In the trunk will be a foldout table, chairs, wineglasses, and a picnic basket, and perhaps a servant. Do it at the zoo and you can pretend you are Robert Redford and Meryl Streep in* Out of Africa. *Hire a chef or a catering service to prepare a special meal for two at your house. Romance seems to be a combination of spontaneity (on second thought, make that planning), privacy, and class.*

273. The 18-Inch Waist

My wife and I recently attended a Victorian ball. In order to have the tiny waist of a Victorian woman, she bought a corset. Surprisingly for both of us, she found the corset not uncomfortable and very erotic. I helped her shop for it and insisted on one that gave her a wasp waist, but did not cover her breasts or hips. She tried the corset before the ball to make sure she would not be too uncomfortable, because I had to lace her in fairly tightly in order for her to fit into the dress. We had a wonderful time at the ball. She looked so sexy I could not keep my hands off her when we got home. She still had her corset on when we started to make love. She experienced multiple orgasms, which she described as the most intense she had ever had. She explained that the pressure from the corset increased the intensity of the orgasms. Since then, we have made love a number of times while she wears the corset. Our usual approach is for me to lace her in as tightly as I can and then for us to go into a social situation that we cannot easily leave. That allows both of us to anticipate lovemaking. In addition, we found that she needs to wear the corset for several hours in order to experience the really intense orgasms. Is there a medical explanation for this?

—L.D., Boston, Massachusetts

The corset is a form of restraint. It inhibits breathing, adding to the physical tension of sex (and the subsequent release). And we thought Scarlett wore them for the eighteen-inch waist.

274. The Combination

The acts that always bring my partners to orgasms are the ones that drive my arousal through the roof as well. They are simple and straightforward! This is my favorite.

As my partner lies on her back I kneel between her legs and slide my hands, palm up, under her soft, sensual buttocks, leaving my thumbs between her thighs. I squeeze her lovely bottom, bring my thumbs together, and use them to gently pull apart the lips of her pussy. I lean down and breathe in the exquisite fragrance before gently blowing over her clitoris. Then I start to lick her clitoris, feeling through the flutterings of her muscles where it excites her most.

As she gets more and more excited, I bring one of my hands from under her bottom and slide two fingers deep into her pussy. I explore the soft, wet walls of her pussy with sensual strokes until I find the most sensitive spot, then I concentrate my stroking there while continuing to lick her clitoris with delight. This combination always accelerates her excitement and guarantees that her hips are soon bucking and pushing hard up into my face, releasing a wonderful flow of juices as she orgasms.

—D.S., the Internet

275. The Stud Puppet

On the very first night of love, we started off by fondling each other for about ten minutes. She unbuttoned my shirt with her teeth while I slowly stripped off her clothes, piece by piece. When we were fully naked, we examined each other's bodies. She directed my hand to her breast. It fit perfectly. I caressed her passionately. I moved my fingers down and began feeling her pussy. She directed my mouth toward her vagina and I licked deep. She gradually pushed my head forward, signaling that she wanted me to lick deeper. She screamed passionately. Then, with a sudden thrust, she grabbed me and threw me backward. She knelt down and started to rub my penis until it was fully erect. She then started to lick it, from the testicles to the tip. She put it in her mouth and violently sucked it. I could tell she was very enthusiastic. She stopped sucking and pulled my dick toward her pussy while wrapping her long legs around me. She was controlling our every move. I felt powerless and uncomfortable. Nevertheless, it was one of the best sexual experiences I have ever had. Until then, every time I had made love with somebody, I was always in control.

—J.N., San Diego, California

276. Talking

At the beginning of the AIDS epidemic, a medical official gave the sound bite of the century. "Because of AIDS," she said, "now when you have sex with a person, you have sex with every person that person had sex with for the past ten years." Forget the epidemiology. The quip supports another truth. I once counseled a reader not to inquire about a partner's past, saying, "Sex is like ethnic food. Enjoy the flavor. Don't ask what went into it."

But people eroticized interrogation. Keith Harary and Pamela Weintraub gave this scenario in *Inner Sex in 30 Days*:

Retire to your erotic refuge with your partner at a time when you feel you will have at least an hour without being disturbed. Then change into loose, flowing clothes and share some fresh fruit, cheese or wine. Before you begin your actual talk, we would like you to remember to tell the truth, to listen carefully to your partner and to be supportive of what he or she says, no matter what that might be. Please do not make your lover feel guilty for any thoughts or feelings and try to avoid feelings of guilt yourself. As you speak, look into your partner's eyes. . . .

[For a first communion ask:] When did you have your first orgasm? Was it with or without another person present? What was your first positive sexual experience? What are your earliest memories about sex? What were your earliest sexual fantasies? What role do these early memories and fantasies play in your sex life? . . . Are there any sexual requests you have not yet discussed with each other? If so, do so now. And be as explicit as possible. Describe the precise way that you perceive your partner while making love. If you have any sexual fantasies you feel are too extreme to actually act on, you may (if you want) discuss these with your partner.

277. The Fog Machine

I am interested in improving my bedroom atmosphere. I would like to create as different an environment as possible, while increasing the sensuousness of the space. I have kept my furnishing spartan (a custom queen-size bed, a nightstand, a receiver and two speakers, and a medium-size flower print). I am thinking that maybe a fog machine stashed under the bed or in the closet would be a good addition. How practical is it? Some other things I've considered include adding a chair or love seat, or hanging a mosquito net or gauze over the bed, maybe draped down over the sides. I was thinking of some offbeat sounds such as ocean surf, jungle noise, undersea animal sounds (dolphins, whales, et al.). Where can I purchase these?

—R.S., Houston, Texas

Whoa. Unless you want to turn your boudoir into a theme park, hold the special effects. You could probably pick up a fog machine from a failed disco or heavy-metal band, but really, now. Outside of inspiring Jack the Ripper fantasies, cold and clammy do not usually add up to erotic. Sounds of waterfalls, oceans, and so forth are kind of hard to dance to (or fuck to), but your local record store probably carries some environmental tapes. We think you might have better results with a selection of your favorite seductive music, something to which earth people can respond.

278. The Body Shot

The body shot is a friendly version of the tequila shot. It requires a willing partner of the opposite sex. First, sprinkle salt on your fingertips. Lick your partner's neck and pat the salt onto the wet spot. Next place the lime, citrus side out, between your partner's teeth. Now follow the usual routine—lick the salt (you have to get all of it), drink the shot of tequila, then suck on the lime.

279. Turnabout

I've been intimate with my lover for three years. We've put a lot of imagination into sexually startling each other. Last night left me with vastly mixed feelings. After a leisurely meal, two glasses of iced white wine, then a hot shower together, she took charge and herded me to bed. There, while I lay on my back, she began fondling my testicles and licking my penis; her tongue was relentless. Soon I had an extremely intense orgasm. She was sucking pleasantly hard, pressing her thumb just above my anus. An instant later, she climbed onto my body and kissed me, spitting my own semen into my mouth. She smeared it all over our lips and tongues and rubbed our faces in the goo. Words fail to describe my feelings about this event. I showed her this letter and she laughed evilly. Sauce for the gander, she says. Your comments?

—J.R., Houston, Texas

How does the song go: "I've looked at love from both sides now"? So your girlfriend showed you what a great blow job feels like from her perspective. What's the problem? But we're intrigued by this game of yours. It sounds like Inspector Clouseau's relationship with his houseboy. What's your next move? Cut a hole in the bottom of a box of popcorn, stick your penis through it, and offer her some next time you're at the movies?

280. Practice Makes Perfect

My girlfriend seems able to reach orgasm in only a few set ways—through masturbation while lying on her back with her legs tightly clenched and through intercourse while lying on her back with her legs tightly clenched. We call it sex in the martyr position. I'm starting to feel inadequate, not to mention bored. We reach orgasm, but we seem to be in a rut. Is it typical for women to have only one kind of orgasm?

—E.Y., New York, New York

One of our friends tells a story about a sign he saw in Kentucky on a back road: CHOOSE YOUR RUT CAREFULLY. YOU'LL BE IN IT FOR THE NEXT 17 MILES. *There are researchers who think that each woman's pattern of orgasm is unique —they call it "orgasmic fingerprinting." Some women have intense orgasms, some mild, some both. There is also substantial evidence that a woman's subjective experience of orgasm varies from situation to situation. It is possible to change. If a woman masturbates in one position, she conditions herself to certain stimuli. Through practice, she can add options. She can learn more subtle sexual sensations*

—by changing hands, by switching from hard, direct stimulation to light stimulation, by rolling over on her stomach, by moving her body against her hand, a pillow, or a doorframe. We've read about women who masturbate on their backs with their legs propped up against a wall, of women who masturbate standing up (pretending that they are doing it in a semipublic place). It is unlikely at first that she will be able to trigger an orgasm from these alternatives, but that is not the point. Intercourse is never as precise as what you do to and for yourself—if you learn to be sensitive to imprecise stimulation, you can accommodate greater variety in intercourse.

281. Secret Sex

As a sophomore (and a virgin) at the University of South Alabama I have been lucky to have the most gorgeous women sit beside me in class. I've noticed something strange. They all cross their legs and move them in a kicking motion. One woman in particular starts making almost silent but very noticeable grunts or moaning sounds. This goes on for a minute or two and the kicks get faster. She then starts moving around, the grunts increase, and then she looks at me, smiles, and relaxes. A few weeks ago, I purchased a book about the art of self-enjoyment. The book, which deals mostly with female masturbation, has a small paragraph dealing with public masturbation. Apparently a woman can have orgasms by crossing her legs and employing constant and rhythmic pressure on her clitoris. Is this true? I'm very attracted to this woman and I would really like to give her my virginity if she is masturbating this way. Obviously, if she is, it means she is attracted to me. Please respond quickly; the semester is almost over.

—P.S., Mobile, Alabama

Is this letter a put-on? Yes, it is possible for a woman to reach orgasm by applying pressure to the clitoral region in a rhythmic fashion. Some women cross their legs, leaving their heel in the appropriate place. We're not sure it means that she likes you or wants to have sex with you. Her smile is the only useful evidence in your scenario. It indicates that she is friendly. Smile back.

282. Broken Condom Cock Ring

My girlfriend and I were experimenting with some condoms when one broke. Rather than take it off, she pushed the rubber ring all the way down my erect penis. After a few minutes, my cock was as hard as a rock. My girlfriend liked it. I liked it. So now I break the condoms before I put them on. So tell me: Did we discover some ancient Chinese sex trick or a brand-new sex toy? Will I hurt myself?

—W.L., Denver, Colorado

What you've discovered is a novel version of the cock ring. The ancient device restricts the flow of blood from an erect penis, which produces a rather enduring hard-on. We've heard of people using everything from leather thongs and rubber bands to napkin rings. This is one of the few sex aids that has a potential downside. If the cock ring is too tight or too hard, it can damage blood vessels. Scar tissue may form, which then deforms the penis. Since the base of a condom is a specific size (about 52mm in diameter) and is intended to fit the shaft of an erect penis without undue discomfort, you may have found a relatively safe version of the cock ring. However, if you were using condoms as a form of birth control, breaking them first is not a great idea.

283. Energy Versus Comfort

Remember the scene in the movie *Nine ½ Weeks* in which Mickey Rourke suddenly plops Kim Bassinger onto the kitchen table and goes into a minute-long sexual rage? Well, I know that having a quickie can be a healthy part of a couple's sex life, but what about the female's state of lubrication? Wouldn't the sudden and energetic thrusting of a penis into an unprepared vagina be painful and cause some short-term soreness for the woman? Should I worry?

J.B., Corvallis, Oregon

The best thing about long-term relationships is that eventually you get to try things you would never do on a first date. Quickies are a prime example. Not exactly what you'd pull on an audition, or serve as a regular diet, but something that definitely makes a statement. In Nine ½ Weeks, *things balanced out—the quickies were intercut with scenes of interminably sensitive foreplay. Good lusty sex is the result of competing appetites, not compromise or politically correct sexual etiquette. Put another way, short-term soreness is a small price to pay for passion and enthusiasm. Imagine the fun you can have comforting the hurt. During a discussion*

*of 2 Live Crew lyrics, a man asked a friend, "How would
you respond if I told you I wanted to break down the walls
of your vagina? Would you feel threatened?" Her answer:
"No. I would like to be there when you tried."*

284. Tattoo

My girlfriend and I are tattoo freaks. We have had
several done and are constantly looking for unusual
designs. The first time we made love we spent the entire
night discovering each other's hidden art. Recently my
girlfriend confessed that she'd always wanted a butterfly
between her legs, so that when she spreads her lips,
behold, a thing of beauty in flight. I must admit that the
idea is intriguing, but how would we go about doing it?
Is there a painless way to apply such a tattoo? Would
any tattoo parlor be willing to accommodate us?
—K.T., San Francisco, California

*According to Spider Webb, tattoo artist extraordinaire,
genital tattoos are fairly common. The process is painful,
but to some that's part of the fun. For a reputable artist,
contact The Tattoo Club of America (203-335-3992). But why
not consider temporary tattoos? These are pressed onto
moistened skin (we'll leave that part to your imagination),
last two to ten days, and can be removed with baby oil, cold
cream, or rubbing alcohol. (Skip that last one for the genital
versions.) They come in a variety of designs, from Harley-
Davidson logos to the usual snakes and lepidoptera. You
can change your gallery of body art periodically. Or take a
felt-tip pen and create your own designs.*

285. Condom Exercises

Whenever I contemplate the idea of using a condom in order to make love to somebody, my penis absolutely refuses to get with it. Intercourse becomes impossible. Is there some help available for this problem?

—G.P., Miami Beach, Florida

You could practice at home. Masturbate with a condom until you know it like the palm of your hand. Try adding lubricants. Turn one of those condoms with ribs inside out so the tiny little fingers stimulate your secret pleasure centers. Become acquainted with a variety of condoms so your anxiety is replaced by expertise. Ask your new friends to put the condom on as part of foreplay—of course, they will be clumsy at first, and that clumsiness may detract from arousal, but at least it's something you're doing together.

286. The Well-Hung Man

Have you ever heard of a woman making love to a man's testicles? During oral sex, my girlfriend sometimes fellates my balls, taking them completely into her mouth. It feels great. Now she wants to try to fit them into her vagina. Is this safe?

—P.C., Milwaukee, Wisconsin

Only if she doesn't plan on keeping them. We've seen this performed in X-rated videos—it creates an on-the-spot ménage à trois. A woman lies on her back and wraps her legs high around her lover's back. She guides the testicles between her vaginal lips—the phrase "two peas in a pod" comes to mind. The shaft of the penis then rests against the clitoris. The guidelines here are gentleness and no sudden moves. This is not the time to put on the Jane Fonda workout tape.

287. Happy Birthday

I'm working on keeping my marriage strong. Our sex life is great and I've made sure we keep it alive. We watch porno films together, admire *Playboy* women together, and share fantasies (I more so than my husband; he has a hard time verbalizing his sexual desires). As a matter of fact, for his twenty-sixth birthday I am planning to rent a hotel room, get a bottle of champagne, and surprise him with a woman from a peel-a-gram place, who for a fee has agreed to do a slow, erotic strip. She will dance for fifteen minutes, bare her breasts (but keep her G-string on), and then leave. There will be absolutely no touching— even if my husband and I are touching under the covers. My best friend, however, feels that I am playing with fire, that it is too much temptation for my husband to put him in a room with a young, gorgeous woman who is dancing half naked and touching herself. Am I playing with fire?

—L.Z., Pittsburgh, Pennsylvania

Yes, but it's your fire. If you're worried, handcuff him to the bed first.

288. The Erotic Bathroom

I once dated a woman who almost never made love in the bedroom. Her ritual was seductive, sensuous, and squeaky-clean. She would disrobe me, take me into a shower, and scrub my entire body. Soaped hands would clean every crevice, every fold of skin around my genitals. And her tongue would follow. Quite often she would bring me to orgasm, then ask me to soap her while she played with the French shower head. The jet of water was as efficient as any vibrator. Other times she would get out of the shower and we would lie on a very deep throw rug to make love. She would grab a bottle of baby oil and ask me to take her from behind. Then, back into the shower to clean up. And that, of course, set up the possibility of more sex. Was she obsessed with cleanliness?

—S.W., Mill Valley, California

Actually, she's onto something. Treat the bathroom as a site for sex and you double the sources of inspiration. Keith Harrary and Pamela Weintraub discuss this in Inner Sex in 30 Days: *"The state of your bathroom environment is an intimate expression of how you feel about your body. It is the room in which you clean your body in preparation for a sexual encounter, and it is often the room in which you will find yourself—for one reason or another—either during a sexual experience or shortly after a sexual encounter is completed. It should therefore be kept scrupulously clean and inviting, using the same sorts of general techniques you used in preparing your erotic bedroom environment. Place a clean and cozy rug on the bathroom floor and make sure there are plenty of clean, large, thick and absorbent cotton towels available at all times. It is often not the most exotic sex aids that make the difference in our enjoyment of a given sexual encounter but, rather, the simple niceties of life."* Keep some candles handy for romantic lighting, a variety of bath oils for slippery sensuousness, a French shower head for getting at those hard-to-reach spots, a loofah for sensitizing skin, razors for pubic trims. Hey, you've been there.

289. Sesame Street Oil

Occasionally, my wife and I enjoy giving each other a massage, which often leads to even more pleasurable activities. We have tried various creams, lotions, and oils. However, we are unsatisfied with most of them. Baby oil is too slippery. Hand creams tend to be absorbed into the skin faster than we would like. All of them taste terrible, which forces us to ignore certain areas that may later require further attention. What do you recommend?

—S.C., San Jose, California

Maybe Paul Newman should come out with a massage oil to match his salad dressing. Try light, natural oils—a mix of almond oil and vegetable oil works wonders. Neutragena has a line of body oils that includes a light sesame formula. Put a bottle of oil in the microwave for a special trick (Grace used to do this on Hill Street Blues*).*

290. The Basics

Why is it that I perform well with one woman and can barely be aroused by another? Or for that matter, why is it that on some weekends with my girlfriend the sex is great, while on others it seems like a chore? What gives? I know it sounds like I'm looking for a secret recipe for great sex, but I just want to be consistent.

—F.E., Chicago, Illinois

Bernie Zilbergeld, author of Male Sexuality, *says that men have basic requirements or conditions that precede good sex: "In their attempt to function like the fabled 'well-oiled machine' men overlook what they already know, that machines themselves have conditions, including being well oiled. When we're made aware of these needs, we don't get upset, we just fulfill them." Review your past. What distinguished great episodes from fiascoes? According to Zilbergeld, a condition can be anything—time of day, how tired or energetic you are, how sick or well you are, how you feel about yourself, how you feel about your partner, what you do, what she does, how much privacy there is, or anything else that makes a difference to you. Think about it. We've heard of women who've reduced the conditions for great sex to an anagram: CERTS—for consent, equality, respect, trust and safety. Sounds like the recipe for a stockbroker or a doctor. Our requirements for great sex might go like this: a shared sense of enthusiasm, fascination, energy, curiosity and/or willingness, playfulness, anticipation (if you aren't looking forward to it, don't do it), a hotel with room service, and so forth. Sprinkle with chuckles, sweat, and saliva. If you attend to the foundation, what follows is frolic.*

291. Play Attention

Sex manuals moved from telling lovers what to do with their bodies during sex to telling them what to do with their minds. In *Male Sexuality*, Bernie Zilbergeld asks men to focus their attention:

When you are kissing, keep your mind in your lips. When your partner is touching a part of you, put your attention in that part. When your penis is being touched or when you are having intercourse, put your attention inside of your penis. Be aware of the fit between the penis and whatever is around it—pressure, texture, temperature and wetness.

292. Play Attention, Part Two

David Schnarch makes attention the goal of great sex. In *Constructing the Sexual Crucible* he describes sex as a window—we see ourselves by what we do in bed. Many people cannot handle the intensity of looking into their lover's eyes, or being there. Schnarch gives this advice: "Practice kissing interruptus. Stop kissing when you feel you are losing contact with your partner or are being tuned out by her or when you sense she is coasting."

293. Echoes

One of my lovers has introduced me to an incredible technique—we call it echoes. He strokes my clitoris with a certain rhythm while fondling some other part of my body with the same rhythm. Whatever area he touches becomes as sensitive as my clitoris. It's like having two erogenous zones singing harmony. Have you ever heard of this technique?

—J.P., Chicago, Illinois

Dr. Bob Schwartz mentions something called "connections" in The One Hour Orgasm: A New Approach to Achieving Maximum Sexual Pleasure. *You can practice the technique during masturbation:*

At some point, apply Vaseline to another place on your body, such as your breast. Begin to tease this part of your body by stroking the outside edge of the area using wide circles. Move slowly toward the nipple or center. Once you reach the center, the nipple should be very excited and turned on. Rub that area with similar pressure and movement as you are rubbing on your clitoris. Try to set up some kind of intercommunication between the two areas. Take your hand off one place and see if you can feel an echo in the other. Keep switching back and forth. It is possible to connect any two areas of your body using this technique. Once you get an area turned on and connected, see if you can bring yourself to the edge of an orgasm using only the secondary area. Do this connecting exercise using as many parts of your body as is pleasurable for you. You might try the middle toe of your left or right foot, your upper lip, your earlobe, the inside of your elbow or thigh and also the arch of your foot.

Try working yourself to a series of peaks, stopping just this side of orgasm. When you finally let yourself go, you should experience a more intense rush. Then try the same technique on your lover.

294. Plaster Casting

I hope you'll be able to tell me a good and safe way to make a dildo using my own penis—erect, of course —as a model. When I'm away, my lover could have a bit of me to keep her company. I need to know what materials to use and how to make a mold.

—S.P., Jacksonville, Florida

You'd be surprised at how often we get this request. One reader wanted to have an elegant dildo made from silver, another wanted a model complete with hydraulics. Why not go the distance and motorize the sucker, with little flames around the corona, rear end jacked up three or four inches, maybe put in a sound system? Okay, here goes. In the sixties, a young rock fan named Cynthia Plastercaster went around making plaster moldings of the penises of rock stars. She tried a variety of materials—obviously plaster takes a while to harden, which turned out to be about the same amount of time it took rock stars to soften. Also, there's nothing like trying to pull pubic hair out of plaster to spoil the moment. She experimented with aluminum foil and hot wax (fill a cylinder with hot wax, insert erection), but hot wax is, well, hot. She eventually obtained the best results using an alginate dental product used for tooth and jaw molds. But who wants to ask dentists for sexual favors?

295. Body Part

A few months ago, you told a reader that he'd be surprised at how often you get requests for information on how to make a dildo from one's own penis. You suggested talking to a dentist about casting materials. There's something better. Bodyparts Lifecasting is available from Flax Art & Designs (800-547-7778). People use it to make casts of their kids' hands and feet, or to make furniture out of reproduced noses, ears, feet, whatever. You make a flexible mold, remove it, then fill it with a plasterlike material for rigid parts. Or you can pour the original mold material into the shape for a flexible part. The mold material is a latexlike substance that feels like soft skin, so supple reproductions of breasts are possible. It sets up fast enough to get all the detail you could possibly want from your subject. The $24 kit has sufficient material to reproduce the largest of individual parts. The company also sells faux-marbleizing kits that allow you to make your rigid reproductions look like fine Italian marble. And it is fun to work with.

—B.T., Atlanta, Georgia

Thanks for the lead. We can see all sorts of uses for creative cloning of body parts. Say you are dating Lorena Bobbitt. It might pay to have a cast of what your penis used to look like. Actually, we ordered some and tested it. It is fun. Ridiculous, but fun. Now, about that faux marble kit . . .

296. The Crème de Menthe Blow Job

Jay Wiseman put together a whole series of sex-trick books, detailing everything from the erotic nature of everyday household items to lusty uses of liqueur. The books are sold in erotic boutiques rather than in bookstores. The following is from *Tricks: More Than 125 Ways to Make Good Sex Better*:

The woman holds a sip of the minty liqueur in her mouth, touches the man's penis to her lips and then parts them slightly, allowing the liqueur to spread over his glans and down his shaft. Then she opens her mouth wider and goes down on his penis and exhales forcefully. Her warm breath on the crème de menthe gives the man an exciting sensation of heat. After that she backs off so that her lips encircle only the head of her lover's penis. She inhales forcefully, and the man experiences an exquisite cooling sensation.

297. Foot Job

Why is it that affectionate or sexual behavior toward women's feet is portrayed as abnormal or kinky? I love massaging my wife's feet or lifting her legs in the air and kissing them while we have intercourse. The feet can bring an erotic aspect to lovemaking, considering how sensitive and ticklish they are. What do you say?

—N.A., Centerville, Virginia

Try doing the 20—it's slightly different from doing 69: you suck each other's toes while fondling each other's genitals.

298. The Rules of an Affair

Women's magazines regularly tell their readers that affairs will improve their marriage. They offer detailed etiquette for conducting dangerous liaisons. The Playboy Advisor rarely brings up the topic, but I couldn't resist running the following set of directions, taken from *Stalemates: The Truth About Extra-Marital Affairs* by Marcella Bakur Winer and Bernard D. Starr:

1. No picture taking or receiving. [Somehow they will be found.]
2. Nothing in writing . . . affairs are allergic to anything in writing. That goes double for diaries, strictly a no-no.
3. No souvenirs. Pack rats as we are, we want mementos of everything. Definitely not a good idea for those engaged in liaisons.
4. Not in the neighborhood or in public. Also, never display affection in public places, no matter how far away from the neighborhood.
5. No thoughtlessness. Just a moment of incaution can bring down the whole world of risk. You may not throw a bra or a panty into the glove compartment of a car.

6. Never in the home.
7. Never forget to keep track. From males particularly comes the suggestion to check all pockets before going home after a tryst. This also includes briefcases. And check your jacket and shirt for stray hairs. Ask your lover not to wear perfumes or scented cosmetics that leave traces. Be careful of presents or phone calls that appear on credit cards or itemized phone bills.
8. Never change your style. For better or worse, each marriage has its own style. Your spouse knows how you act and respond. Don't change your style because you feel different.

Of course, break all of these rules—with your spouse —and you have the ingredients of a great marriage. Keep souvenirs. Make phone calls. Leave the underwear in the glove compartment. Drench yourself in her scent. Leave traces.

299. The Three-Eyed Turtle

As we were writing this book, rumors of a new sex trick began to ricochet around the air waves of America. Shock jocks and talk show hosts began to phone the Advisor asking if I had ever heard of "The Three-Eyed Turtle." I hadn't, and then proceeded to have as much fun as anyone trying to imagine a trick that would merit that name. Did it involve thrusting one's penis between your partner's thighs from behind so that she could look down and pretend that the erection was hers? One friend thought it involved a certain mystical faculty, perhaps best expressed by the French art director who said, "Even though I let them sit on my face, I keep one eye open." I finally tracked down the source: On *Love Phones* Dr. Judy Kuriansky frequently describes an uncircumcized penis as a one-eyed turtle. During one show she suggested that a couple rub the head of the penis against the clitoris (the second eye) while observing the results in a mirror (the third eye). Her crew dubbed the technique the Three-Eyed Turtle.

300. Heat

I don't know if they still make it, but back in college my lover and I used to play with self-heating shaving cream. The stuff would heat up a few seconds after application—a major rush when applied to certain erogenous zones. Nowadays, we sometimes play with Ben-Gay or Tiger Balm—as long as you don't get it on really sensitive skin (inside the vagina), it's a real turn-on. Sort of like playing with finger paints that catch fire. I had one lover who was into special gels made with cinnamon or peppermint oil that would heat up if you breathed on them. Be sure to wash off the oil before moving to intercourse.

—N.B., the Internet

301. Clothes Make the Man

My husband and I have a pretty good relationship. My sexual drive seems to have increased, and I have been asking him to do more things than he usually does. I especially enjoy making love to him when he is wearing a shirt unbuttoned to expose his hairy chest, or a vest without a shirt. I would particularly like to make love to him while he's wearing a suit coat without a shirt—or anything else—on. I wonder if other women like their men to wear certain articles of clothing while making love?

—D.B., Helena, Montana

Chaps? Spurs? We understand your fascination with skin on the other side of business attire: We're a little jealous of women's business suits. Or is that aroused? Removing the middle layer can be incredibly erotic.

302. More Masturbatory Imagery

My wife and I have found a position in which we can both have an orgasm every time. She lies on her back and I lie on my side perpendicular to her so that she can masturbate during the act. My problem is that she is so inhibited about her masturbating and her facial expressions during orgasm that she covers her head with a pillow. What can I do? When I ask her why she is embarrassed, she says she doesn't want to talk about it. There's nothing like seeing a woman's facial expressions while she's having sex. We've been married more than two years: It seems to me she would be comfortable with me by now. Help!

—G.W., Atlanta, Georgia

Have her wear a blindfold, so she can't see you watching. You can sit across the room and watch her while she masturbates. You can reach out and touch her. She won't know where the next touch or breath is coming from. In short, turn her anxiety into erotic suspense, then tell her what it's like to watch her face, the cords in her neck as they stand out, the arch of her back, the blur of her hand. Take a Polaroid of her face as she comes. We've seen photo exhibitions of people's faces caught in the act of coming. It is one of the most powerful and intimate images on earth. And very disturbing to some.

303. Mirrors

It seemed inevitable that after a sexual revolution, we would pause to assess the history of sex. Is there anything new under the sun? Richard Zacks collected vignettes of vice in *History Laid Bare*. Seneca's account of a notorious libertine, circa A.D. 10, presents a rather clever use of mirrors:

Take Hostius Quadra. His sex life was so notorious it was featured in a stage play. . . . Hostius' lewd behavior wasn't limited to one gender; he lusted after both men and women. He ordered mirrors made that magnified reflections so that a finger appeared greater in length and thickness than an arm. Those secret acts (the ones that if accused of, every man denies), he experienced them not only in his mouth but with his eyes. . . . And he wasn't satisfied with just simply watching, he surrounded himself with mirrors strategically placed so he could divide up his sordid deeds and rearrange them. . . . "Let my eyes too share in the nasty fun and be witness and judges of it," said Hostius. "By means of mirrors, let even those acts be seen which the contortions of our bodies hide from sight, so that no one can claim I don't know exactly what I'm doing. . . . Let me, in my lust, see organs larger than they are and marvel at what I'm able to handle!"

304. Top-Level Sex

My fiancée and I were on the way back to her dorm when we realized that it was after midnight on a school night. (Visitors of the opposite sex are not allowed in her dorm after midnight.) We decided to pull into her college's parking garage. We drove up to the top floor and found it deserted. We backed into a spot and she climbed over to the driver's side. The sex was wonderful, and the fact that there was a chance of being caught heightened the pleasure. After enjoying ourselves immensely, she sat back in the passenger's seat, and we dressed. We could not believe that we got away with it. Not a single car drove by the entire time. Then, out of the corner of my eye, I noticed a security camera pointed directly into the car. I guess we got caught after all.

—N.B., New Orleans, Louisiana

305. The Kinky Keyboard

My wife found it uncomfortable to sit on the edge of the table while having sex. We were both quite surprised at how easy it was after having spur-of-the-moment sex in my home office with her sitting on my keyboard. The keyboard seems to work like one of those foot-massager thingies, except on your ass!

—P.A., the Internet

306. Hitchhiker to Heaven

My favorite sex trick is the "Thumb Ride." This entails gently slipping a thumb into the lady's vagina from behind. Flexing the thumb places the pad of the thumb almost exactly on the G spot. (I don't care what others may say, the G spot definitely exists. Stimulating it properly always has the desired effect.) Gently manipulating the G spot with the pad of the thumb elicits multiple quivering orgasms every time. These climaxes, often very wet and very loud, can last up to an hour or until the lady begs for mercy, whichever comes first.

—M.H., the Internet

307. The Airplane

I am sure that many people can claim this space as one of their accomplishments, but I have told this story to enough curious ears that I know there are plenty of interested "virgins" out there. Sometimes where you do it is more important than anything else. My girlfriend and I had planned to fly from L.A. to Boston for a family reunion. Right up to departure time, I kept asking her if she wanted to try the old fool-around-in-the-bathroom stunt. She never really said yes because I think she was skeptical that it could be pulled off, but once we were in the air, I was determined to make it happen. Since the trip was five hours long, I made sure we got a blanket and pillows, and we bundled up just after liftoff. Surveying the plane, I noticed there were three or four bathrooms at the rear. Our seats were eight rows from the back, so I could see two of the bathroom doors. I was very happy that we had one row of seats to ourselves. Somewhere over Las Vegas, I slid my hand onto the top of her thigh. She wanted to look nice for the relatives, so she wore a very nice sundress for the trip (which, in my mind, was only going to make my quest just that much easier). Within a minute, my hand got under the dress and I had my hand on bare skin. I figured that if I could get her "started" at her seat, she'd be more receptive to trying my stunt. I caressed her warm inner thigh, making ever-increasing circles, lightly brushing against her underwear as my hand passed by her treasure. The entire time we were cuddling, we both had our eyes closed and were under one blanket in an attempt to keep people from noticing what we were doing. Pretending to sleep also helped keep the flight attendants from bothering us. My girlfriend was very receptive to my actions and started to breathe a little heavier. On the last circle, I softly planted my hand directly on her panties and gave her a soft but solid massage. This really got her going. It was obvious that the conversations leading up to the flight had planted some erotic ideas in her head. It was taking very little coaxing to get her aroused. The challenge now was to keep her from moaning in an otherwise quiet airplane.

She has always liked her clit rubbed in small circles with just the right amount of pressure, so I decided to do this to put her emotions into high gear. She was beginning to show signs of weakening, as her breathing was starting to get loud and she was finding it difficult to stay in her seat without squirming. A quick look to the bathrooms showed me that no one was in line. Finally, I whispered to her, "Why don't you go to the bathroom and lock the door. I'll be by in thirty seconds and knock three times." She didn't even hesitate. She stood right up and walked quickly to the rear of the plane. It was a good thing the plane was bouncing a little, because she was having a hard time walking. I watched which door she went in, and then I waited. I knocked three times, and from inside the little room, she unlocked the door. I walked through the door and slid the lock back in. The bathroom was about twice the size of a phone booth, with a small shelf and a mirror on one side. I decided to scoot past her and sit on the shut toilet seat. The first thing I noticed when I sat down was her panties hanging from the coat hook, and before I knew what was happening, she took her right hand and placed it just under my nose. From the warm aroma on her fingers, I could tell that she had been busy with herself while she waited for me. I looked at her with a big smile, and she said that if I had waited any longer, she would have finished without me. I instantly dropped my pants to my ankles so that she could sit on me. It was a little difficult because there wasn't enough room, so I spun her around, putting her back toward me, which left her facing the door. This position proved to work best given the cramped conditions. I lifted her dress as she sat down on me. I slid right into her and we were both in heaven. As she slid up and down on me, we could watch ourselves in the mirror—what a great added surprise that mirror was! We were both so close to climaxing before we got started that it didn't take long for us to finish. We were both very proud of ourselves for joining the Mile-High Club. All that was left was for us to quietly return to our seats.

—K.S., the Internet

308. Imagining

In 1986 Marc and Judith Meshorer published *Ultimate Pleasure: The Secrets of Easily Orgasmic Women*. *Playboy* excerpted the work, presenting this tidbit:

"Before an evening when I'll probably make love, I'll try a dress rehearsal in my mind. I know where I want to get, the end result—in the bed under the covers with the little light on."

—Rita

When easily orgasmic women think about making love, hours or minutes in advance of a sexual encounter, their thoughts may be only thoughts—vague feelings or ideas without specific words or pictures consciously attached. Usually, these thoughts are of a positive nature and assist sexual arousal by reinforcing the endearing or positive qualities of a partner or a situation. . . . Preparatory imaging takes place before a woman has physical contact with a partner or, in some instances, during the early phases of lovemaking.

Kate takes special care with her grooming and bath. When I'm going out, I pamper myself. I enjoy a change of dress from the everyday suit I wear to the office. I soak in the tub and I light the candles and I take my wine in and I do the whole bit. I scrub and perfume and touch myself from head to toe. I work myself over, and I exercise. I take pleasure in the feelings of my body. By the time my date picks me up, I feel so good about myself that even if he doesn't desire me, I desire me.

309. The Backyard Pool

My wife and I have discovered the following to be quite erotic: We have a wading pool for our backyard. It's not just a source of fun for kids. In the summer, when the nights are warm, we have, on occasion, shed our clothes and frolicked in the shallow pool. Of course, we make sure the back porch light is off.

—B.M., the Internet

310. Saran Wrap

When Marabel Morgan encouraged women to greet their husbands at the door in something sexy, one wife supposedly dressed in cellophane—only to discover that her husband had brought the boss home for dinner. But there are more serious sexual uses for the shiny stuff. In Alex DeRenzy's X-rated classic *Babyface*, a woman wraps a man in Saran Wrap—leaving only his erection free. The cellophane completely immobilizes her victim, and she proceeds to exact a specific revenge that we will leave to your imagination.

311. Just Do It

Talk radio is a phenomenal source of sexual information. Dr. Judith Kuriansky—aka Dr. Judy—has entertained listeners for years as the media psychologist on New York's Z100 radio's *Love Phones*. She collected the best advice—including the following—in *Generation Sex*:

For women wanting to change their position masturbating, it sometimes helps to use a vibrator, because the orgasms come more quickly and reliably, so you don't get discouraged and the new position is rewarded more easily.

Katherine is most creative. "I pour jelly on the corner of my bed and rub against it. Sometimes I use whipped cream between my legs and then take it off with my fingers and eat it. Sometimes I insert the feet of my doll inside me. Once I put a condom on a banana."

312. Pop Rocks

I always liked to eat Pop Rocks when I was little. Now I have found a better use for them. You can place them on your partner's vagina before oral sex. They will snap, crackle, and pop her into a nice big orgasm. She can return the favor by placing one in her mouth before performing fellatio.

—D.M., the Internet

313. Strokes

"Different strokes for different folks" is a fairly popular slang expression; one of my friends claims it is based on historical evidence. Apparently, some scholar devoted his life to a study of the average number of strokes needed to bring women of other nations to climax. Have you heard of such a study?

—H.H., Roanoke, Virginia

Yes, from a Navy recruiting officer. Actually, there was a study of that sort conducted in the eighteen hundreds by Jacobus Sutor, a surgeon in the French army. (Men stationed at hardship outposts learn to pass the time in odd ways.) Sutor's findings were published in 1893; L'Amour aux colonies *included such erotic recipes as "Nine times shallow and one time deep" for Hindus, "Ten times shallow and slow, ten times deep and quick" for Japanese (repeat if necessary or possible), and, finally, "Forty times in and out will bring the majority of Chinese women to a climax," although the more responsive ones will get off after "eight shallow thrusts and two deep ones." Why the emphasis on shallow strokes? Masters and Johnson point out that the outer third of the vagina is the area most sensitive to stimulation—as a woman becomes excited, this area becomes engorged with blood and tightens around the penis, while the inner two-thirds of the vagina expand. Shallow strokes, therefore, may tease and arouse a woman as much as or more than deep thrusts. So hire a coxswain and conduct your own study.*

314. Waterworks

I have found a way in which to enjoy myself between lovemaking sessions. I wait until my boyfriend has gone to work, then I deadbolt the door. Then off to the bathroom I go. First I take a hot shower and get relaxed, then the excitement begins. I turn on the faucet and get a good, steady powerful stream of water going and, in a sitting position, with my feet on the edge of the tub, I center it on my clit. I don't think receiving oral sex from any man could even come close to the excitement, because it is so intense, stimulating, and ecstatic.

—S.K., Clearwater, Florida

315. Carnal Camera

Kevin Campbell discovered that camcorders are the sex toy of the nineties. To guide people who can't even program their VCR through the joys of making your own erotic movies, he wrote *Video Sex*. Although it looks like a tech report, the book is actually a great sex manual. Consider the following:

In personal erotic videos, seeing your partner's face while making love or reaching orgasm will probably be one of the most exciting subjects you can tape. This is where your own videos will be much more arousing than commercial adult videos: you get to see your lover moan, writhe about, and say your name, rather than watch strangers copulate. Quite often it's difficult to get a good visual vantage during sex, or maybe you close your eyes. Video gives you the opportunity to watch what you do and see how it affects your partner. Facial close-ups leave more to the imagination . . . videotape her expression during oral sex and orgasm.

Remember Ellen Barkin's facial expressions in *The Big Easy*?

316. Moonlight Interruptus

There are many places that can be erotic, and stimulating for great sex. And I've found that switching the place is *the* most sensual thing there is, especially if you don't plan it. One of the more entertaining places I've had this experience was in the woods . . . sorta. My girlfriend and I were just walking through the Cleveland Metroparks (I'm from Cleveland, going to school in Syracuse) and we stopped at an observational lookout. The view was wonderful, and since it was night, the moonlight hit her face like nothing I'd seen. It was a beautiful sight.

She got this feeling in her, and she pulled down my pants, and proceeded to orally stimulate me. Now, she's done this before, but something about the fact that we hadn't planned it and that we could be caught was wonderful. It was the best she had ever done and the best I had ever had. . . . Unfortunately, a couple slammed their car door not fifty feet away and we had to stop. But I will always remember that.

—K.F., the Internet

317. Sizzling Sausage Santa Fe

I've noticed an odd trend in sex manuals: The culture has come full circle. The new books discuss sex in the context of marriage, just as John Eichenlaub did years ago. Patrick T. Hunt gives us the opposite of the ice trick in *Red Hot Monogamy in Just 60 Seconds a Day*:

Step One, heat up a tube of K-Y Jelly by holding it under hot water.

Step Two, squeeze tube and introduce the lubricant into your "love oven."

Step Three, have your partner slowly introduce sausage.

Step Four, repeat till meat is sizzling.

318. Erotic Torture

Some authors present a singular, surefire sex trick. Naura Hayden's *How to Satisfy a Woman Every Time and Have Her Beg for More!* elevated teasing to an art form:

> Teasing is a form of sweet torture, for both of you. And we all—both men and women—have a touch of masochism within us. The act of surrender, which is the most beautiful part of orgasm, is surrender in love to the one you love. . . . Now if you want to try something that is sexually incredible, but incredibly difficult to do, get to the point you're both seconds away from orgasm, and stop. Just stop cold. And resume several hours later, or the next morning. Holding back like that will triply excite you when you resume your lovemaking, and you'll both be so sensual and so ready that when you start over again with the teasing, you'll both be tortured with desire, and by the time you gently tease her clit with your penis, she'll be screaming for you to enter her, and when you start gently putting your penis in her a half-inch at a time, she'll be pleading, begging for you to go in more. And when you both have your orgasms, the experience will rock you both like you've never been rocked before.

319. Fingers

Sexual techniques are a Rorschach: Each person brings a different meaning to the interaction of flesh. But if you put your attention into the tiny acts of sex, you can find out truly astonishing things about yourself. Elaine Kittredge, author of *Masterpiece Sex: The Art of Sexual Discovery*, gives this account:

He took my hand quite comfortably. Throughout the whole ride he gently caressed it, tickled it, slid his finger suggestively in and out of little crevices, and was generally exceedingly erotic in his suggestive symbolic gestures. It is certainly an art, holding a hand well and turning someone on by such a subtle touch that no one else on the train knew what was happening. And he did it just because it was fun, and he knew he could, and he knew I would understand and not make a big deal of it.

It made me think again of why it is so thrilling to have my lover put his fingers in my mouth, or why, now that I have overcome my shyness, when I am very erotically enjoying a kiss, I like to put my finger in his mouth or in between our mouths so I can feel both my finger and our tongues at the same time, or why I like to put my fingers on my genitals so I can feel his tongue there at the same time. It is wonderfully erotic because of the symbolism. There is no other way I can show my male desire to enjoy entering any other way. And maybe that's why slipping the end of a wet finger gently into his anal opening while I have his gorgeous cock in my mouth is such a thrill for me, and obviously for him.

320. Crescent Moon

I was watching cable one night and saw an erotic music video that was really quite hot. It showed a couple making out in the front seat of a convertible, top down, under a streetlight. The scene was clearly choreographed to show off the girl's body—you could almost hear the director off-camera telling the male to position himself above and away from the girl, just so the camera would catch the beautiful lighting. The next time I made love I held myself above my girlfriend. I reached out and traced the very outside edge of her body. My touch was lighter and slower than a tickle; she just shivered. And when she ran her fingernails down my side it was like connecting a live wire from my hips to my head. When you're floating in sensation, the move sort of reminds you where the edge of your body is—and that's a rush.

—N.B., Chicago, Illinois

321. For Women Only?

Why is it that if a woman leans over the dinner table and whispers, "I'm not wearing any underwear," it's considered very erotic, but if a guy whispers the same thing, it's considered weird?

—R.P., Los Angeles, California

It's just one of those gender things, the same one that says that if you come home and find a trail of blouses, shoes, stockings, and lingerie, it's an invitation to paradise. If your lover comes home and finds a shirt, tie, pants, and shoes on the floor, it's an invitation to an argument. If a date comes back from the ladies' room and presses her underwear into your hand it's love. If you come back and do the same, it's laundry. If you want equality, better to discuss it before you go out. The hottest sex takes some planning: Agree to strip your inner garments before going out on a date, then spend the whole night looking for a spot where you might get away with a little groping. You might find time for a little fondle here, a little nuzzling there—and there's always the car to come. The notion that it might happen at any moment puts a sexual throb over the whole evening.

322. Talking Holy

What is the secret of great sex—intimacy or anatomy? Barbara De Angelis has explored the interplay of the soul during lovemaking, yet even in her writing you find moments of extreme arousal. This is taken from *Real Moments for Lovers*:

There is a time during sexual lovemaking for silence, and there is also a time for words. Words add a whole other dimension to lovemaking. They create yet another channel across which your love can flow. While the movement of your body and the sounds you make communicate to your partner's body, words communicate your passion to your lover's brain. And it's the brain that controls all the pleasure centers in your body. The words you share when you make love turn on your brain and help it turn on your body. . . . Many people avoid using words during sex because words of desire make them feel too naked and exposed. I can be feeling that my lover's touch makes me hot, but if I say to him "your touch makes me so hot," now I am sure that he knows, and now I am more vulnerable. My words give him power over me, that power that comes from knowing his seduction has been successful, from knowing that I want him.

323. Reveille

I sometimes wake my lover with fellatio. It is perhaps the only time when I take complete charge, when he does not feel the need to reciprocate or get hung up on the need to be active and male. There's no distraction, no baggage from the day. All the foreplay is mine. It is a remarkably gentle encounter. Sometimes I notice that he is in the last stages of a dream, that he has an erection, and I simply take him into my mouth. I suck gently, or just let him feel the warmth of my lips. The fun part is trying to guess when he first becomes conscious of my activity: He has on occasion pretended to sleep right through it all, waking with reports of a phenomenal dream. Other times he responds to subtle rhythms with rhythms of his own. It's a little harder to reverse the roles—but early-morning oral sex works for everyone.

—A.Q., the Internet

324. The Subway Strap

This may sound weird, but it works. My girlfriend and I started fooling around with different positions for oral sex. I would stand by the bed. She would lie on her back and take me down her throat while touching herself. Sometimes I would reach down and add a hand, to find that she was truly excited. I asked if giving oral sex turned her on; she responded that it was the view, and the feel. So we tried positions where I simply straddled her chest while I stroked myself and she touched herself. That worked. Sometimes we will just lie side by side; she will use a vibrator or her hands— all the while hanging onto my erection for all it's worth. When she's finished, she will then turn to complete my pleasure (often reaching a second orgasm). Other times, she just borrows it for a while. Is this weird?

—P.K., New York, New York

She's found—let's count them—about four different uses for your arousal, all of them powerful. Is this what it means to be a sex object? Every erection does not have to be sheathed in a vagina. Avoiding penetration allows your partner a great deal of control. We think we've heard this called a one and a half, something to do with a partial daisy chain.

325. Up on the Roof

I went to school at the University of Miami, Coral Gables, Florida. I had a girlfriend who confessed to having a fantasy for having sex in public places. I was initially very hesitant about this, but after talking this over at length, we reached a compromise. We decided to find a spot which would put us in a position so that we could view the world around us, but nobody could see us. After a lot of experimentation with deserted library aisles, computer lab late at night, et cetera, we chanced upon a place that seemed perfect: the roof of our apartment building!

We would typically go out late in the evening, where we would make out until we both were horny. Then we would come back to our apartment building and head for the roof. I would arrange for a sleeping bag, some munchies (we found grapes to be great turn-ons), and lots of tissues to wipe ourselves with. On the roof we would find a spot that would face the road, where people would be walking about, and other apartment buildings. There were lots of people around.

The roof itself was very dark, so none of these people could see us (or so we hoped). We would take our clothes off (we kept a blanket handy, in case somebody decided to visit the roof, too) and watch the people below. We were typically very horny by this time, and we would get right to work . . . Our favorite technique was for me to lie on my back and she would come over me in the 69 position. We would be close to the edge so that we could look down easily, then we would eat each other until we would have to put our hands over our mouths to stop from moaning and groaning. Then she would mount me and fuck my brains out.

She loved to lie down facing the road, and have me right behind her, entering her from the back—and taking it real slow. I don't know if many people have tried this, but it sure was fun.

—S.H., the Internet

326. The Lovers

Have you rented Louis Malle's classic film *The Lovers*? Jeanne Moreau spends an entire night with a young man. It is one of the most languid, sensual encounters ever filmed, and it is a catalog of elegant techniques. The two meet outside Moreau's house and go floating down a river on a rowboat (the craft seems to respond to their every move—kind of like a waterbed in reverse—and it creates a very private place away from the gaze of husband and friends). When they finally make love, Moreau traces words of love on her partner's back. (Try that with your mate— see if she can guess what you are spelling.) But the best secret? Before she leaves the house, Moreau draws a bath of cool water, something she says she does on every hot night. After making love, she and her lover slip into the water for another session of lovemaking. The following morning the young man takes a sip of the bathwater to quench his thirst.

—R.P., the Internet

327. The Fantasy Man

I read about this guy in *The Tennessean*. He would call women pretending to be their boyfriend. In a whisper he would tell them to leave the door unlocked and to get into bed blindfolded. The he would walk in and have sex with them. He apparently succeeded with three women, some of whom enjoyed several sessions before discovering his ruse. According to the story, he also talked women into masturbating in front of open windows. If it works with strangers, think of what it will add to your relationship. I've parked outside my girlfriend's house with a cellular phone and arranged private shows. Very hot.

—T.R., the Internet

328. The Glory Hole

This is a classic orgy trick, a cliché in porn films, and an ongoing attraction in some underground clubs. In the cuter versions, several men hide behind a curtain and poke their erections through tiny openings. They have to guess if the mouth that is fellating them belongs to their wife, and the fellatrix has to guess which erection belongs to her husband. In certain clubs, strangers simply push their erection through holes in a partition: They accept anonymous pleasure from people on the other side. You don't need a crowd to enjoy this: Hang an old sheet in the basement, or knock a hole through a room divider.

The anonymity and suspense—coupled with the isolation of the genitals—is a complete rush.

329. Outside/In

My wife fell asleep on the couch the other night. She'd stayed up late to watch something or other. When I woke and noticed her absence from our bed, I went down to fetch her. I kissed her, then, as she started to wake, I unfastened her clothing. I performed oral sex, then replaced my tongue with two fingers. I kissed her thighs while my fingers moved in and out. I tried to imagine what she felt like: As her hips began to writhe I whispered, "This is making me come." I experienced an orgasm, coming on her belly, then inserted myself. When she came, I came a second time, even more intensely than the first. Have you ever heard of a multiple male orgasm?

—N.B., Chicago, Illinois

Yes. And you seem to have stumbled upon a phenomenon several readers have described. An erection holds more than one orgasm, and it seems to know the difference between inside and outside. Many people can go from an oral sex orgasm to an intercourse orgasm without losing their erection. The second orgasm is always more intense. That you so identified with your partner's responsiveness may be another clue—since you thought your first orgasm was actually hers, there was still the masculine one left.

330. The Cabana

The last time I visited a nude beach, I befriended a woman. She had one of those little semicircular tents, and she invited me inside. With the flap of the tent closed, we could see to the outside through the cloth—but it was impossible for anyone to see in. We then proceeded to get hot and heavy—and we finally made love. Nobody saw us—and it was very exciting to have sex in an open, yet concealed place. We have since become good friends.

—S.D, La Jolla, California

331. Washday Miracle

Making love on top of the washing machine while it is on the spin cycle can be an unusual experience. The vibrations from the machine can be very erotic. If you want to add heat to the buzz, try the dryer.

—G.F., the Internet

332. The Whitewater Orgasm

I once had great sex in a raft going down a river. We had to be inconspicuous, since there were other rafts on the river. We timed intercourse so that we climaxed going through a rapid. It really added a touch of excitement and thrill.

—D.A., the Internet

333. Fire and Ice

In your request for sex tricks, you referred to a movie in which two women used an ice dildo. I actually prefer Popsicles—cherry—myself. The stick makes them easier to handle and keep under control. It also adds to the experience if your partner is blindfolded with her wrists lightly bound the first time you try it. That way it will be a complete surprise. A little note here—there will be an initial shock. My last girlfriend almost tore the headboard off my bed when I tried this one. After that, "Fire and Ice" was her favorite pastime. First the heat of my kiss, then the kiss of ice.

—J.C., the Internet

334. Ménage à Popsicle

First I took a bandana and affixed it as a blindfold. Then I visited the freezer and found two Popsicles. I took the tip of the orange Popsicle and touched it to her clit. She giggled and squirmed and guessed, "Ice?" I said nope . . . keep guessing. As I stroked it along her outer lips and back up to her clit, she said she couldn't guess. That's when I took the entire Popsicle and thrust it into her. She gasped and ground her hips against my hand. I slowly pulled it out and inserted it into my mouth. Her juices were dripping by now, and so was the Popsicle. It tasted heavenly. She said, "Do that again, please!" through excited gasps. I did it again, and again she squirmed in excited pleasure. This time she said, "What the hell is that?" I put it to her lips and said, "Taste." While she sucked on the orange Popsicle, I continued with the second Popsicle. Eventually I had to clean up: kissing her, working my way up her thighs to her pussy. The tastes combined to make a sweet tangy flavor that was like nothing I'd ever tasted and it was simply delicious. She orgasmed like an avalanche. It seems that the cold from the Popsicle had numbed her inside, but when my tongue entered her, it heated her up so fast she couldn't control herself.

—T.S., the Internet

335. Hot Tub Ice

Here is one that always gets 'em going. If you and your partner have access to a Jacuzzi/hot tub, get yourselves a bucket of ice and hop into the hot water. Grab a piece of ice and begin rubbing it all over your partner's body. Start on the backside and work your way all around to even the most sensitive of spots. Use your imagination and explore your partner thoroughly. Find the spot that gets them the most. If done properly and erotically, your partner is sure to reach orgasm. Now reverse roles and repeat the process.

—M.M., the Internet

336. Drumming

Most people know how sensitive nipples, male and female, are to stimulation. We all like to wrap our lips around our partner's nipples, tease them with our tongue, nibble at them, pull at them, pinch them, suck on them, too. Something a friend demonstrated on me as being very effective is to simply bounce a finger or thumb against one or both nipples. It sounds silly, but it heats me up to an incredible pitch. This works with the penis, clitoris, or anus, too.

—D.P., the Internet

337. Cool Breeze

It is natural to think of stimulation as being tactile— that is, to stimulate a nipple, we touch it in some way. Temperature, especially cold, is also an extremely effective tool for stimulation. Something I like to do is select some part I want to stimulate, such as nipples or genitals, and lick that part for a moment. Then, once the area is wet, I can either suck in air while close to it or move back a few inches to blow on it. The air provides an evaporative cooling effect that can really drive a partner wild. An alternate means of cooling is to suck on crushed ice, especially if it's mixed with a drink high in alcohol content, before licking the area to be stimulated. Alcohol provides greater cooling effect than water does. Trust me, it's fun.

—D.P., the Internet

338. Nerve Dance

The body has many areas that are sensitive and useful as erogenous zones—above and beyond the obvious lists of breasts, nipples, penis, scrotum, clitoris, vulva, vagina, and anus. In fact, at any place where two major body groups are joined together—the crease between thigh and vulva, the crease between thigh and abdomen, behind knees and inside elbows, wrists, and armpits, between the butt cheeks, the base of the throat, the ears and behind the ears, and the spine—there is a surplus of nerve endings. The feet, hands, and ears have the greatest number of nerve endings per unit of surface area, and therefore have extremely high erotic potential. This includes fingertips, palms of the hands, between the fingers, tips of the toes, soles of the feet, between the toes . . . The real question is, what can we do with all that potential? Something that really works for me is to have my partner lie naked, face-down, while I start somewhere. Usually I start at the feet. I mention the part I want to focus on, then I use my fingertips or the backs of my fingernails to lightly brush along the area. After a moment I follow it up with my tongue or lips. If it is her toes, I spend some time with her toe tips, caressing, licking, blowing on their wetted surface. After a short time, but not too short, repeat the same process with another part of her, perhaps the soles of her feet, the base of her neck, or her ears. After half an hour of this my partner on one occasion, no lie, was all set to rape me.

—D.P., the Internet

339. The Transition

In two great films—*She's Gotta Have It* and *Like Water for Chocolate*—the heroines prepare for sex by lighting hundreds of candles. The directors probably did it for the image, but they are onto a sex secret. There is a phase of sex that precedes foreplay—it's called the transition. Sex is an altered state; it is not "the real world." How lovers bridge the distance can make or break a relationship. Some lovers employ rituals—the clipping of fingernails, the loosening of hair, the sharing of a bath. Some employ music—putting on a favorite tape, perhaps engaging in a slow dance before moving to the bedroom. Others say, "Let's hit the video store and see if there's anything new." We know couples who pull out travel brochures (planning trips or remembering past vacations) before enjoying each other. If you aren't having sex as frequently as you want, it may be that you haven't left room for the transition.

340. Creative Cooking

My girlfriend and I call it the Banana Method. First we microwave two ripe bananas until they are refreshingly warm. Then we break out two pounds of Hershey's baking chocolate. We melt that in a fondue pot, then dip the bananas into the chocolate. We like to tickle each other with the bananas, then lick each other clean.

—J.C., the Internet

341. Playground Sex

Make love on a seesaw (the missionary position works best, although face to face in a lotus position is a close second). You may have to fiddle a bit to get the balance right, but if you succeed you'll find that when you thrust, the balance changes. Ride the thrust, then pull back. It can be silly (a sudden change can catapult you off the seesaw) or very seductive—a slow-motion ballet.

—E.S., the Internet

342. The Leash

As near as we can tell, the Marquis de Sade was the first person to come up with a book of numbered sex tricks. *120 Days of Sodom* is profane, perverse, and of almost no use to the modern lover. In fact, we can relate only one of the tricks. In it, a woman uses a long cord to masturbate her partner:

A man ties a long cord around his prick; then he gives the free end to a girl, who holds it against her cunt, steps over it and begins walking away. While contemplating her ass as she walks, the man ejaculates; by this time the cord has been pulled quite taut.

343. Double Blind

A little tip I saw in a movie: Each partner has to wear something to cover his or her eyes. You'd be surprised at how much of sex is based on visual clues. When you can't see a thing, you discover a different way to read your partner's body. Touch comes out of nowhere: You feel like there are more than two people making love.

—A.M., the Internet

344. The Vacuum

I have found that masturbating using a vaccum cleaner with the extra-wide hose attachments is quite stimulating. The air blowing past the exposed penis is subtle; some models can cause the foreskin to flutter.

—G.E., the Internet

345. The Belly Rub

A technique that I'm particularly fond of using, and that gets many requests, goes as follows:

1. Have your lady friend relax on the bed, floor, or kitchen table on her back.
2. Begin to perform oral sex on her at an easy pace.

3. Once she has been warmed, insert your middle finger into her vagina.
4. Next, slide your finger upward until you are nestled against her clitoris.
5. With a controlled force, push your finger toward her clitoris and at the same time begin to lick and suck on her clitoris with more force.
6. While you are trying to accomplish the above, place your other hand upon her tummy just above her pubic bone and with a bit of force push downward in a circular rubbing motion.
7. Next, observe your partner's ass raise off the bed.

—C.M. the Internet

346. Over the Edge

In a porn film called *Sodomania 9*, one scene re-creates a fantasy of sex in prison. The prisoners push their erections between the bars of a cell and a female prison guard plays with them. You might be able to re-create the feel of contained sexual wildness with a bannister or chain-link fence (since we doubt most homes have basement dungeons). The scene culminates with an absolutely outrageous ménage à quatre in which two inmates have sex with the guard's feet, putting their penises between her toes. Consider other parts of the body for sex—the armpits, between the thighs, between her feet. Find the softest skin on her body, and the hardest. Some writers have suggested making love to your partner's hair. Clear this with her first.

347. Olive Oil

One thing I found that makes for great fellatio sex is plain old olive oil. You coat your lover's erection with a light layer of Virgin Italian and go to work with both hands and mouth. He won't know where your lips end and the oil and hands begin—it involves the entire penis and is as close to deep throat as he's likely to get.

—L.P., the Internet

348. Sexual Charades

You don't need whips and chains to create a dungeon. In Andrew Blake's *House of Dreams*, an actress standing in an empty room simply puts her hands above her head, as though suspended from the ceiling. Posture alone can invite all the power and drama of dominance and submission into a scene. Indeed, some observers of the S&M scene in New York now say the letters are shorthand for "Stand and Model." Can you put your body through an alphabet of desire? Hands behind the back? One arm across your eyes? Walking on or falling prostrate from your knees? Back against a door frame, half in, half out? Play this as a game with your partner: Have her guess what you want her to do, simply from the position of your body.

349. The Lick Trick

On a recent flight I overheard two women in the row in front of me giggling lasciviously about something I think they called the Lick Trick. Have you ever heard of it?

—M.L., Astoria, New York

Sex therapists in California recommend the technique to patients, but why should they have all the fun? The Lick Trick is a technique to hasten either a man's or a woman's orgasm when performing oral sex. Instead of using steady tongue pressure or swirling moves to pleasure the clitoris or head of penis, you tease the undersides of these organs with light little licks about once every ten to fifteen seconds. Maybe less is more: The trick usually produces a quick, intense orgasm.

350. Tiffany Tease

I've seen photos of nipple jewelry—women wearing chains from breast to breast, or rings through each nipple—that are a major turn-on. My girlfriend likes the look but doesn't want to do anything as permanent or as painful as piercing. Is there a safe alternative?

—D.E., Dallas, Texas

Check your local erotic boutique. There are several creations that use adjustable loops. A woman can tighten an elastic band around an erect nipple and then suspend something eye-catching—feathers, tassels, chains, or silver balls that knock against each other, sending constant stimulation back to the breast. Erotic jewelry is closing the gap on lingerie. We've even seen elegant clitoral clips—they look like paper clips that surround the hood of the clitoris. Just the thing for those lazy days around the house.

351. Giggles

When my boyfriend found that by caressing my clitoris correctly he could make me giggle as I climaxed, he got hooked on making me laugh in bed. Now he teases me with feathers. We've tried different types, but the best is a fan made of feathers that when kept closed makes an amazing tickler. My boyfriend uses it on me from head to toe. Of course, certain parts get special attention. He holds my arms over my head and runs the fan from one nipple to the other and back again until I'm nearly breathless, then across my ribs and belly down to my clitoris. This is followed by the hottest boffing session you could imagine. If there were anything better than this, I'd never live through it. The one problem is that the combination of body oils, perspiration, and other natural juices eventually destroys the feathers. Washing the fan stiffens them. Do you have any advice on how to keep my ticklers soft and pliable? Finding feathers with the right features— soft edges with a stiff spine—is difficult. Any suggestions?

—K.O., Miami, Florida

Sure. Use a live bird; it is self-cleaning. Just kidding. We've heard good reports about badminton shuttlecocks (the nonplastic variety), volley birds (a Brazilian toy), and feather boas. When you find something that works, buy a dozen. For cleaning, take your fan to a professional dry cleaner and ask him to hand-clean it with perchloroethylene (the recommended solvent for ostrich feathers).

352. Upside-Down

My girlfriend and I have discovered a terrific yet simple addition to our lovemaking. She lies on a sofa or a bed with her head hanging down. The rush of blood and slight dizziness add to the strength of her orgasm. Have you heard of this phenomenon?

—E.S., New York, New York

Sure. Next time you're at a garage sale, look for a pair of gravity boots. Then hang your lover upside-down from a chinning bar. If you have the upper-body strength, you can try a vertical 69.

353. The Speedometer

Dr. Helen Singer Kaplan, a leading sex therapist, provides a neat exercise in self-awareness in *PE: How to Overcome Premature Ejaculation*:

Rate the degree of your sexual excitement (not your erection) on a subjective scale which runs from zero to ten. Zero is when you are feeling absolutely no excitement at all and ten is when you reach orgasm. You should have been stopping penile stimulation when you were at about eight and a half. If you tried to go until nine and a half, you went a bit too far, and if you stopped at four or five, you ended the stimulation a bit too soon. Remember, the aim of this program is not to keep your excitement down until you want to come. That is no fun at all, and besides, that doesn't work. The objective is for you to learn to ejaculate while staying at the intensely pleasurable sexual plateau stage which precedes orgasm, and to be able to relish the delicous sensations of being highly aroused instead of trying to hold back. During real-life intercourse, most men stay somewhere between five and seven, except for brief peaks of eight or so, until they are ready to go all the way.

354. The Ninety-Degree Tilt

My girlfriend likes to make love standing up. She claims the position allows her as much control as the much-touted woman-on-top position, plus it has the added benefit of pressure: With her back to the wall, she enjoys the feeling of being caught between a rock and a hard place. I must admit, the position does have its advantages—we have made love in showers, in telephone booths, in self-service elevators, in hallways, and in restrooms on airplanes. When we experimented with bondage, instead of tying her spread-eagled on a bed, I handcuffed her to a chinning bar and did it in a doorway. As long as she gets off on it, I'm willing to go along, but it's gotten to the point that we almost never do it in bed. My question is this: Is she weird?

—D.D., Detroit, Michigan

No. She's just the right size. Perpendicular sex gives excellent front and back pressure, plus the added downward tug of gravity is a different thrill from normal thrusting. And there are plenty of precedents. Think of Al Pacino frisking Ellen Barkin against the wall in Sea of Love. *Think of Mickey Rourke and Kim Basinger against the wall in* Nine ½ Weeks. *Think of Michael Douglas and Jeanne Tripplehorn starting against the wall in* Basic Instinct. *Next time you have her back against the wall, ask her to wrap her legs around your waist. Rock gently.*

355. The Source

Anaïs Nin's *Delta of Venus* is a virtual catalog of tricks. As a writer, Nin set herself the goal of noticing what went on during sex. Every paragraph is a lens that focuses erotic energy. Keep a copy by the bedside and read it aloud to your lover. There are great lines ("What part of you wants me tonight?") and highly charged scenarios. In one story, a husband tells his sexually frigid wife that he has given her an aphrodisiac —just as she leaves for a movie date with a lady friend. She becomes obsessed with the possibility of sex:

> She had heard of women caressing each other in the movies. A friend of hers had sat this way in the darkness of the movies, and very slowly her companion's hand had unhooked the side opening of

her skirt, slipped a hand to her sex and fondled her for a long time until she had come. How often this friend had repeated the delight of sitting still, controlling the upper half of her body, sitting straight and still, while a hand was caressing in the dark, secretly, slowly, mysteriously.

In another story, an artist keeps a model in a constant eroticized state:

Once he asked one of the painters for his warm pipe. The man handed it to him. He slipped the pipe up Bijou's skirt and laid it against her sex. "It's warm," he said. "Warm and smooth."

Bijou moved away from the pipe because she did not want them to know that all the Basque's fondlings had wetted her. But the pipe came out revealing this, as if it had been dipped in peach juice.

Every time I read about a new sexual trend—for example, the recent stories about "Do-Me" feminists using dildos on their boyfriends—I turn to Nin and find the same action. She is the master.

—N.B., the Internet

356. On the Twelfth Day of Christmas

In December 1994, *Playboy* published "Stocking Stuffers," a collection of sex techniques guaranteed to bring joy to the holiday seasons. Trickster emeritus Jay Wiseman shared his expertise with our readers, offering such gems as the following:

In *Tricks* we discussed a technique called Climbing the Mountain. For him, by her. It's usually done with the man lying on his back. The woman sits or kneels beside him or between his legs. Take his penis in one hand and gently, sensuously caress it for about ten seconds, then give it one quick up and down stroke. Repeat the sensuous caressing for about ten seconds—perhaps doing slow up and down strokes, perhaps doing other things that feel good—then give his penis two quick up and down strokes. Repeat the sensual caressing, then give three quick strokes. Then more caressing, followed by four quick strokes. Then more caressing, and five strokes. You get the idea. You can vary the caresses—adding twists or tongue or scratches—for each verse of the song. See if he can last for twelve full strokes. This same trick works for oral sex—his and hers.

357. Dressing Sexy

In the movie *Don't Look Now*, Donald Sutherland and Julie Christie have torrid sex in a Venetian hotel. The director intercut scenes of lovemaking with scenes of the two dressing afterward. It is strip poker in reverse. Next time you undress your partner, pay particular attention to each belt, buckle, button, or clasp. Then, when you are done, carefully reclothe your lover, containing the wildness, reminding him or her that you will return.

358. Dogging

Have you ever heard of something called dogging? A British porno magazine that I read recently mentioned it—it seems to have something to do with public sex.
—M.B., Raleigh, North Carolina

Dogging is the English term for a sport in which couples have sex in cars while people watch. Specific parking areas have been designated for dogging, and couples identify themselves as performers by turning on a colored interior light. Etiquette pertaining to group sex clubs, such as no touching or extraneous noise, often applies.

359. Reach Out and Touch Someone

My wife and I have a rather unusual problem. She likes to hold my penis a lot. Not just as a prelude to sex, but also during nonsexual times. I can't remember the last time we watched television when she wasn't holding it. I go to sleep, she's holding it. I wake up, she's holding it. When we read the Sunday newspaper together, she takes her hand off it only long enough to turn the page. Sometimes I get irritated and tell her to lay off, but she says that it's like holding hands. What can I do?

—W.B., Burbank, California

If she wants to cuddle, she should do it with a different part of your anatomy. If she wants to make love, have her use a different part of her anatomy—say, her mouth.

Editor's note: There is a sex trick here, we just didn't notice it the first time. In a short story by Anaïs Nin, a woman artist drawing a young man notices that he has an erection. Over the course of several days she goes from sketching it, to stroking it, to grazing it with her lips, to intercourse. The man wonders each day how much farther she will go. You can introduce this kind of tension into your own relationship. Make teasing a week-long process. Don't let a day go by without touching your partner's genitals—but don't consummate the act. See what happens when you finally cross the line.

360. Monitor Sex

My girlfriend and I would like to videotape ourselves having sex. Where's the best place to position the camera?

—P.J., Chicago, Illinois

Put your camera on a tripod and run a cable to a video monitor or television set. You can view yourself during sex, which may prove hot or hilarious, and change positions accordingly. A longer cable will allow you to separate the camera and monitor so that the finished product doesn't look as though you filmed in a TV repair shop. Other tips: Play with the lighting. Kill the overhead and try a few desk lamps as substitutes for spots. Experiment with colored bulbs—especially red and blue. And don't point all your lights right

at the bed. Indirect lighting can create alluring shadow ef-
fects. Candlelight adds to the mood and creates both motion
and mystery. And once everything is ready, go slowly. In-
stead of simply going at it, start clothed and slowly disrobe
each other. The camera may be stationary, but you can still
move—not just by doing the old in-and-out, but by moving
in and out of the frame and in and out of the light, and by
performing under the covers as well as on top of them. Tan-
talize and tease the camera.

361. Chain Drive

Everyone knows how to use a string of pearls during sex, right? In case you don't, take a string of pearls. Draw them slowly across your partner's body. The series of bumps can tantalize a clitoris, tickle a nipple, and create an interesting rhythm on the nerve endings around the anus. Well, my lover and I discovered that you can do the same thing with a length of chain. She owns a waist chain of fairly heavy silver. One night I started dragging it across her body, with great effect. We've since added one neat twist, not possible with pearls. We put the chain into a bowl of hot water—the temperature and texture create a double thrill.

—B.N., Chicago, Illinois

Some cultures take the textured touch to extremes. Some
Japanese men have small stones embedded in their pe-
nises. You can achieve a similar effect by putting small mar-
bles or ball bearings into a condom or by buying a French
tickler at your local erotic boutique.

362. Fur Mittens

Everyone has seen *Goldfinger*, the James Bond movie where he gives a beautiful woman a rubdown with a fur mitten. If you haven't done this yet, you should. But don't stop there. Think of the feel of other materials. We've read about some lovers who use rough canvas garden gloves, leather driving gloves, and heavy rubber electrician's gloves. Try out combinations. (Our favorite: leather workout gloves that leave the tips of the fingers free.) Doing this in front of a mirror can add a visual dimension.

363. Pepsodent

A woman who ran a massage parlor once passed along this tip: If you think fellatio takes too long, simply squeeze some Pepsodent toothpaste into your mouth before going down on your lover. Something about the taste, the suction, or the ingredients will accelerate his response and cause him to tear out his hair, and generally surrender to the cosmos.

364. Don't Move

Most men want to drive their partners wild in bed. They thrive on responsiveness, on reckless abandon. But the opposite can be just as thrilling. We once saw an erotic video in which a man begins to perform oral sex on a woman seated in a chair. Looking up at her, he says, "Don't move." The command is as effective as real restraints.

365. Singing

My girlfriend and I were in a hotel room in New York. We'd turned the television to MTV just so we would have a soundtrack for our sex. She was on top of me, moving in slow circles on my erection, when one of her favorite songs came on. She began to sing and move her body in time to the music. It was not just a visual treat—every trick every singer has ever used on a microphone, she used on my erection. The muscles inside her clenched in time to the music, and in sync with the emotion of the lyrics. Imagine the hottest dance you've ever seen in a disco, then put yourself beneath it.

—L.W., Chicago, Illinois

The Playboy Advisor's Bookshelf

Problem Solvers

For Yourself: The Fulfillment of Female Sexuality by Lonnie Garfield Barbach (Signet, 1975)

For Each Other: Sharing Sexual Intimacy by Lonnie Barbach (Signet, 1984)

Sexual Solutions: For Men and the Women Who Love Them by Michael Castleman (Simon & Schuster, 1980)

Allies in Healing by Laura Davis (HarperCollins, 1991)

Becoming Orgasmic by Julia Heiman and Joseph Lo Piccolo (Simon & Schuster, 1986)

PE: How to Overcome Premature Ejaculation by Helen Singer Kaplan (Bruner Mazel, 1989)

Ask Me Anything by Marty Klein (Simon & Schuster, 1992)

Generation Sex by Dr. Judith Kuriansky (Harper Paperbacks, 1995)

The Sexual Self by Avodah K. Offitt (Lippincott, 1977)

Night Thoughts: Reflections of a Sex Therapist by Avodah K. Offitt (Congdon & Laites, 1981)

Constructing the Sexual Crucible by David Schnarch (Norton, 1991)

Stalemates: The Truth About Extramarital Affairs by Bakur Winer and Bernard D. Starr (New Horizons, 1991)

New Male Sexuality: The Truth About Men, Sex and Pleasure by Bernie Zilbergeld (Bantam, 1992)

Pleasure Guides

Total Sex: An Illustrated Guide to the Ultimate Pleasures of Physical Love by Dan Abelow (Success, 1976)

ESO: How You and Your Lover Can Give Each Other Hours of

Extended Sexual Orgasm by Alan P. Brauer and Donna Brauer (Warner, 1983)

Video Sex: Create Erotic & Romantic Home Videos with Your Camcorder by Kevin Campbell (Amherst Media, 1994)

The Modern Guide to Sexual Etiquette for Proper Gentlemen and Ladies by Tom Carey (Turnbull & Willoughby)

The Joy of Sex by Alex Comfort (Crown, 1972)

More Joy by Alex Comfort (Crown, 1973)

Cosmopolitan's Love Book (Cosmopolitan Girl Library, 1972)

Real Moments for Lovers by Barbara De Angelis (Delacourt, 1995)

The Marriage Art by John Eichenlaub (Dell, 1962)

New Approaches to Sex in Marriage by John Eichenlaub (Wilshire, 1980)

How to Satisfy a Woman Every Time and Have Her Beg for More by Naura Hayden (Bibli O Phile, 1982)

Inner Sex in 30 Days by Keith Harary and Pamela Weintraub (St. Martins, 1990)

Xaviera's Supersex by Xaviera Hollander (Signet, 1976)

Red Hot Monogamy by Patrick T. Hunt (CCC Publications, 1994)

The Sensuous Woman by 'J' (Dell, 1971)

On The Safe Edge by Trevor Jacques (WholeSM, 1993)

Nice Girls Do by Dr. Irene Kassorla (Playboy Press, 1980)

Sex Self-Taught by Don R. King (Nelson Hall, 1977)

Masterpiece Sex: The Art of Sexual Discovery by Elaine Kittredge (Optext, 1994)

Hot Monogamy by Dr. Patricia Love and Jo Robinson (Dutton, 1994)

The Sensuous Man by 'M' (Lyle Stuart, 1971)

Mystical Sex by Louis Melman (Harbinger House, 1990)

Ultimate Pleasures: The Secrets of Easily Orgasmic Women by Marc and Judith Meshorer (Dutton, 1987)

Fantasex: A Book of Erotic Games for the Adult Couple by Rolf Milonas (Putnam/Perigee 1983)

The Total Woman by Marabel Morgan (Revell, 1973)

Sex Drive by Donald Norfolk (Headline, 1994)

Oral Sex Made Easy (International Sex Institute, 1982)

Terrific Sex in Fearful Times by Brook Peters (St. Martin's, 1988)

The One Hour Orgasm by Dr. Bob Schwartz (Breakthrough, 1992)

The Art of Sensual Loving by Dr. Andrew Stanway (Carrol & Graf, 1989)

The Clitoral Kiss: A Fun Guide to Oral Sex for Men and Women by Kenneth Ray Stubbs, with Chyrell V. Chasen (Secret Garden, 1993)

Romantic Interludes: A Sensuous Lovers Guide by Kenneth Ray Stubbs, with Louise-Andrée Saulnier (Secret Garden, 1986)

Right Brain Sex by Carol G. Wells (Prentice Hall, 1989)

The Good Vibrations Guide to Sex by Cathy Winks and Anne Semans (Cleis, 1994)

Tricks: More Than 125 Ways to Make Good Sex Better by Jay Wiseman (self-published, 1992)

Tricks 2: Another 125 Ways to Make Good Sex Better by Jay Wiseman (self-published, 1994)

Scholar Sex

The Complete Kama Sutra translated by Alain Danielou (Park Street, 1994)

The Book of Sex Lists by Albert B. Gerber (Carol, 1981)

The Complete Marquis de Sade translated by Dr. Paul Gillette (Holloway House, 1966)

Sex A to Z by Robert Goldenson and Kenneth Andersen (Pharos, 1989)

Sexual Practices: The Story of Human Sexuality by Edgar Gregersen (Mitchell Beaszley, 1982)

The Dutchess of Windsor by Charles Higham (Pyramid, 1975)

Oragenitalism by Gershon Legman (Bell, 1979)

The Destroying Angel by John Money (Prometheus, 1985)

Simons' Book of World Sexual Records by G. L. Simons (Pyramid, 1975)

The Playboy Book of Forbidden Words by Robert Anton Wilson (Playboy Press, 1972)

Love Around the World by Lailan Young (Hodder & Stroughton, 1987)

History Laid Bare: Love, Sex, and Perversity from the Ancient Etruscans to Warren G. Harding by Richard Zacks (Harper, 1994)

The Cliterati

Pleasures edited by Lonnie Barbach (HarperPerennial, 1986)

Erotic Interludes edited by Lonnie Barbach (Plume, 1995)

Herotica edited by Susie Bright (Down There Press, 1988)

Herotica 2 edited by Susie Bright and Joanie Blank (Plume, 1992)

Herotica 3 edited by Susie Bright (Plume, 1994)

Ladies' Own Erotica by the Kensington Ladies Erotica Society (Simon & Schuster, 1984)

Delta of Venus by Anaïs Nin (Simon & Schuster, 1979)

Slow Hand: Women Write Erotica by Michele Slung (HarperCollins, 1992)